CU00793593

To Keep the Guide Law

A look at Guide Fiction Stories.

By Heather Talbot

County archivist, Girlguiding Worcestershire

Heather Talbot .

Making that all-important Promise.

Published by Aspect Design 2009
Malvern, Worcestershire, United Kingdom.

Designed and Printed by Aspect Design
89 Newtown Road, Malvern, Worcs. WR14 1AN
United Kingdom
Tel: 01684 561567
E-mail: books@aspect-design.net
www.aspect-design.net

ISBN: 978-1-905795-22-2

Introduction

To Keep the Guide Law

This book is my contribution to mark the Centenary of Guiding, which will be celebrated between September 2009, marking 100 years since the date of the first appearance of girls at the Scout Rally held at Crystal Palace, and October 2010.

Centenary Year will be a time to celebrate our past, mark our present and look to the future.

My book is not intended as a history of Guiding or a learned document, but for entertainment and amusement.

I hope it will be of interest to enthusiasts of Schoolgirl Fiction as well as to my fellow Archivists in Guiding who work in many counties, and also of course in Ireland, Scotland and Wales. I hope too that it will appeal to Guides of all ages, past and present, perhaps introducing some to a world of books, which I frequently inhabit!

Most of my source material consists of the books themselves, together with photos and drawings from the Guide Archives both in Malvern and the County of Worcestershire. I acknowledge reference to 'The Encyclopaedia of Girls' School Stories' by Sue Sims and Hilary Clare for brief biographical details, to the Guide Association for the Promise and Law, and to Mrs Joan Firth, who kindly gave me permission to use her carefully researched Bibliography.

I appreciate the kind permission of David Grugeon and his brother with reference to the use of books by Ethel Talbot, their great-aunt. The portrait of Mrs A.C. Osborn Hann is used with the permission of Lutterworth Press.

Extracts from 'The Chalet Girls in Camp' by Elinor Brent-Dyer and 'The Abbey Girls Play Up' by Elsie J. Oxenham are re-printed with permission of Girls Gone By Publishers. I am grateful for help in the early stages from John R. Hogarth and Ann Pestell for lists of Guide stories, and from the late Heloise Collier, our CHQ Archives Consultant, who put me in touch with Mrs Firth. I am also grateful to Margaret and Karen, the past and present CHQ Archivists, to Christine Harris and others who have supplied me with books.

I would dedicate this to the fourth generation of Guides in my family, with thanks to my friends, who have given me encouragement, and to my husband for his constant support and technical help.

Contents

Chapter 7

Chapter 8

Chapter 9

Chapter 10

Chapter 11

Chapter 12

Chapter 13

Chapter 14

*Jean Milward, Gretchen Ward, and Mrs. Kidson,
cooking in camp 1940s*

General Introduction
A brief history

The Boy Scout Movement dates from 1907 when Baden-Powell ran the first experimental camp on Brownsea Island. The Girl Guide Movement dates from 1910, but its true beginning was in September 1909, when a number of girls wanting to be Scouts joined the parade of Boy Scouts at the Crystal Palace Rally. Wearing adapted Scout uniform with long skirts and staves they joined in the ranks for inspection by the Scout Founder, who was surprised to see them there. The girls wanted to be Girl Scouts, but Baden-Powell was not keen on this although he agreed to think about it. His decision was to set up a separate organisation for girls, to be called 'Girl Guides', naming it after a famous Corps of Guides in India, a resourceful body of men. He asked his sister, Agnes Baden-Powell, to adapt his book 'Scouting for Boys' making it suitable for girls.

She took over the new venture for him, becoming its President and finding interested friends to take on other positions.

Who was Baden-Powell and how did he have the genius to start a Movement which has at its heart an unfashionable moral code and which has survived into the 21st Century?

Born Robert Stephenson Smyth Baden-Powell on 22nd February 1857 he was at times known as 'Stephe', 'B.P', and even at Charterhouse School, at his own suggestion, as 'Bathing Towel!'

He came from a large family of ten children, the sixth son and the eighth child. His father, the Reverend Professor Baden-Powell, an Oxford Professor, died when Robert was only three years old. His strong-minded mother brought her sons up to be self-reliant and very able men. Robert went to Charterhouse School at the age of thirteen, taking part in many of the activities available, although not a good scholar. With his brothers he had sailed, gone on expeditions and learned to live in the outdoors. At school he stalked birds and animals, studying nature, but was also a clever mimic and an artist who drew equally well with either hand!

He entered an open exam for commission into the Army and did brilliantly, coming so high on the list that he received his commission very quickly after leaving school. At the age of 19 he was serving in India as a Second Lieutenant and his military career continued there and in South Africa culminating in the famous Siege and Relief of Mafeking. There from October 1889 the small garrison under Baden-Powell held out until relieved on May 17th 1900 and Baden-Powell became a national

hero. During the siege he had used boys to carry messages and collect information and these were the ideas on which he later based the book 'Scouting for Boys', He returned to England in 1903 and worked on this scheme, trying his ideas out at the camp on Brownsea Island from 1st to 8th August 1907. From this small beginning the Boy Scout and Girl Guide Movements evolved.

He was knighted by King Edward Vll in 1909 and in 1920 at the first Jamboree in Richmond Park became the Chief Scout of the World. Nine years later he was given the title of Lord Baden-Powell of Gilwell.

Lord Baden-Powell with Lord Somers at Eastnor, Whitsun 1937.

Agnes Baden-Powell, like her brother, was accomplished in many fields and had a circle of friends to whom she looked for help in the new enterprise of Girl Guides. These ladies networked before the word was invented and it is to them and many other ladies, who at that time could have chosen other outlets for their energy, that Guiding owes its growth. There were certainly girls calling themselves Scouts in a number of places before 1910 and before there was a Girl Guide Headquarters where they could register. The first company registered was 1st Pinkney's Green, also called 'Miss Baden-Powell's Own'.

In the early days the cradle of Guiding was in the Girls' Boarding

Schools and their Headmistresses and former pupils became the first Guide Commissioners, some only just after leaving school.

These were the early days, the real pioneering days, and these were the women who organised the Girl Guide Movement, forming committees and enthusiastically making it possible for girls to learn to aim high and to succeed in whatever they put their minds and skills into. In the original Scheme for Girl Guides the aim was for character training. to give all girls the ability to be better mothers and guides to the next generation. As developed by the Guide Association this was to benefit generations of girls of all ages, helping them to achieve their potential in a single sex organisation, but having fun and friendship. This still attracts girls and women in an age of very different values, when they also have demands on their time and energy never dreamed of all those years ago.

Lieutenant General Sir Robert Baden-Powell was on a cruise on RMS Arcadian touring the world to visit Scouts early in 1912, when he met Olave St.Clair Soames. She was on the voyage to the West Indies with her father. Romantically, and to her surprise, the Founder recognised her as he had seen her two years earlier walking her brown and white dog in a London park, and for her part, she had written to tell her mother 'that the only interesting person on board was the Scout Man'. They fell in love and became unofficially engaged. He was then aged 54 and Olave was 22. The official engagement was announced in 'The Sphere' in September 1912 and this was followed by marriage at Parkstone. Olave had enjoyed a very sheltered upbringing in a family that moved house constantly, but always living the country life of a privileged family. She took up active work for Girl Guides in 1916, becoming Sussex County Commissioner and from then

Lady Baden-Powell with Miss Alice Baird. Five Counties Rally, Hereford, 1928.

11

on, besides bringing up her three children, her energy and leadership was at the heart of the growth of the Guide Movement and support for her husband in the Scout Movement. She became Chief Commissioner and in 1918 became Chief Guide and it as this that she is remembered.

Lord Baden-Powell died in Nyeri, Kenya, in January 1941 and his much loved wife continued faithfully in his work until her death in July 1977.

Anyone who met Lady Baden-Powell, even in her later years, will never forget the meeting, or the sense of fun, the enthusiasm and sheer love of Guiding that radiated from her.

Girl Guide Fiction

Since the start of the two Movements in 1907 and 1910 many books have been written featuring Scouts and Guides. Besides a large quantity of non-fiction books and manuals, too many to list, there are also many adventure and schoolgirl/schoolboy stories with Scouting and Guiding subjects.

The very first book of Girl Guide fiction, published in 1912 by Nisbet, is 'Terry the Girl Guide' by Dorothea Moore. She was born in 1880, the daughter of a clergyman, and educated at Cheltenham Ladies College. She ran her own Guide troop for many years and had her own experiences to draw on. The foreword of this particular book was written by Agnes Baden-Powell, Lord Baden-Powell's sister, the first Guide President.

In the foreword she writes 'Here is a book giving the key to all the mysteries of the Girl-Guide pursuits.

This book was written very early on in Guiding, before the First World War, and is set in a Girls' Boarding School, precisely the type of school from where the early Guide companies came. Women who had been among the pioneers in education staffed these schools. They were certainly the strong-minded women who could give a lead in the Girl Guide Movement.

Chapter 1
Be Prepared

'Be Prepared' is the motto Lord Baden-Powell, the Founder of Scouting, gave to the Boy Scouts and then to the Girl Guides. The letters B.P. serve as a reminder of the Founder.

In the manual Girl Guiding, first published in 1918, he gave an explanation of the motto as it applied to the Guides, stating that they should be ready for any kind of duty. They should know in advance what to do, having already practiced, for any sort of accident or work that might be involved. Referring to the 1914-1918 War, the Great War, he paid tribute to the splendid work of many women, but pointed out that many more could have done this, had they 'Been Prepared.' They could have prepared themselves in advance, by learning to do more outside their schools or homes. He considered that this was the aim of Guides, learning as they played games or camped, to make themselves useful in other ways.

It is as relevant today as in 1910 or 1918 - always be ready in any situation to help others, to anticipate problems, to deal with them and to prepare to meet all the varied challenges of life. However, then as now, Scouting and Guiding provide the opportunity to do all this while making friends and having fun.

The lessons Scouting and Guiding teach are not taught in a school or college, but through games and challenges at meetings and in the great outdoors.

'This is how you row a boat!' Guides in camp at Borth.

Terry the Girl Guide - by Dorothea Moore

The story is that of 12-year-old Terry Vaughan, opening with her 5 brothers, all Scouts, going off to camp for the last fortnight of the holidays. She is left behind wishing she wasn't a girl and could go too! Faced with spending the time with her father, Major Vaughan, a former soldier, she suggests that they should have a holiday on their own. Eventually they travel to St. Yvenec in France, hoping to find out what has happened to a Lieutenant Arden, who had saved Major Vaughan's life when they were soldiers. Major Vaughan knows that Arden married a French nurse called Fleur-de-Lys but his own wife's death has prevented him from making contact earlier and when he has written, his letters have been returned unopened.

They discover that only the daughter of the Ardens, her-self Fleur-de-Lys Arden, is still alive, being cared for by a local lady, the village shopkeeper in whose house they had booked rooms. After the near drowning of Fleur-de-Lys in an incident when a playmate dies, they take her back to England to live with them.

A tall figure came through the water.
(Book frontispiece)
Major Vaughan rescues Fleur-de-Lys after Terry has run for help.

Major Vaughan then sends both Terry and Fleur-de-Lys to a boarding school, the Manor School. The book then has much in common with many of the school stories of the period. The girls take time to settle in and find that they are thought of as only first formers who can have no opinions of their own! The girls become friends with Penelope Calcot, a loner who writes fairly excruciating poetry and whose father is a 'power in the press'.

The Manor School pupils are excited to receive a visit from an 'Old Girl', Mary Mainwaring, who has topped her successes in the scholastic world by her bravery in India. Having married a Major Eytoun, she has lived in India as a soldier's wife until a siege in which she behaves heroically, defending her husband and saving the day. Terry, greatly impressed by this story, has been invited by Hendrika Hanson who is having tea with Mary Mainwaring and others in the Headmistress, Miss Warwick's room, to go to her study after prep to hear more about 'IT' (Mary's heroism). She goes along with her two friends and after knocking on the door is invited in by the heroine herself. After an awkward time while waiting for Hendrika Mary asks if she can help them. Terry plucks up her courage to ask the question:

"Oh, please, Mary Mainwaring - Mrs Eytoun, I mean - it's fearful cheek, I know, but if you would tell us something, ever so little, about IT. We - oh, it would be most awfully good of you!" she burst out, running half her words into each other in her eagerness, "We're only First Form, of course, but -"

Mary Mainwaring stopped and became rather pink. Then she looked down at Terry, and Terry felt emboldened to go on.

"Hendrika was going to tell us a little; she was truly."

Mary was still pink, but she was smiling, and she put her arm round Terry very kindly. "There isn't much to tell. I wonder what you want to know," she said. But she sat down, on the window seat this time.

Lys looked at Penelope, and Penelope at Terry. It fell to Terry to answer that last question too. Terry was hot, but she got it out, though almost in a whisper. "How you - did it!"

Mrs Eytoun gave a funny little choky laugh. "There wasn't any doing - that's what people don't understand - at least nothing special. Just the everyday things - in a setting, which wasn't quite everyday. But the setting doesn't really count, you know."

The three, facing the heroine about whom all England has been talking, stared blankly. Terry voiced the general bewilderment when she gasped, "Everyday things!"

Mrs Eytoun smiled again; but she looked as though if she had not smiled she might have cried.

"Yes, everyday things - nursing, cooking, keeping places clean," she said - "every-day things which I often muddled dreadfully. It doesn't make a good nurse or sick-cook of you to be popped into a hill-fortress with people's lives paying the price of your mistakes; the making has to come first."

There was no doubt now about the tears in Mary's eyes; she could not go on for a moment. Penelope took the opportunity to put in her word. "In books you always know if you're a heroine."

The remark had the good effect of bringing back the smile to Mrs Eytoun's face, "Yes, you do, and isn't it convenient! she said brightly. "But I'm afraid poor everyday people have to learn." Even Penelope could not contradict Mary Mainwaring, but she had a way of sticking to her point. "Not a real, proper heroine?" she asked.

Then Mary Mainwaring said something, which she seemed to find it rather an effort to say. "I wonder what you children mean by a real, proper heroine - somebody to whom the chance has come of doing something splendid and who has taken that chance? But I very much doubt if it is opportunity that makes the heroine; it is the opportunity coming to people who are ready for it. If Grace Darling had not known how to handle a boat, all the wish to help them in the world could not have saved those poor drowning people, could it?"

Terry later on thinks hard about this and suggests to the others

"I've been thinking, couldn't we learn to do some of the little things that would be wanted if the big thing came? Girls can't be Scouts I suppose but Hendrika says that Gytha (the Head girl) knows all about the Girl-Guides, because her sister is a Captain in them. They get ready: they won't have to keep out of the way because they're no use if the big thing comes."

Terry, being only a lowly first-former, approaches Gytha and at first is turned down. However Gytha later changes her mind after being impressed by a newssheet they have written. The school does not accept contributions for the official school magazine from the first form and the first-formers have made up their own newssheet, called 'Vox Populi'. Among the articles Penelope has written one supposedly by a famous cricketer, Mr Armstrong, headed 'Sports and the Empire'. This gives advice to girls on sport concluding with the comments:

"Because it doesn't matter whether you do anything great yourself, as long as you play up all you're worth for your House. That's how it's meant to be with the Empire - you've got to play up for it, because thinking imperully is putting the Empire first, and yourself second, Imperullism wants a lot of practice at the Nets too, and one of the Practice-Nets, and a jolly good one, is to be a Girl-Guide. You can be one inside, even if the big ones don't want to fuss about enrolling you."

The Head-girl, Gytha, accepts this contribution for the 'Manor School Magazine' and as editor writes that she is 'glad to see the spirit of practical patriotism in the Lower School, and that intending applicants for the Girl-Guides might apply to her!' Although she still considers the Girl-Guides a nuisance she writes to the Headquarters in Buckingham Palace Road for them and wants to know how many will join. Most of the First form and a few from the second want to join but they agree to start in a small way with a Lone Patrol. Their first problem is how to acquire some uniform:

It was fortunate that it was still so early in the term that pocket money had not had time to grow very scarce. Terry sent round the hat, and there was an anxious consideration of ways and means, accompanied by some arithmetic, mostly wrong, on the back of an exercise book. Cissie Duncan, who was practical, suggested that ordinary blue serge skirts would do, and that you could make the two flap-pockets out of any blue stuff and sew them on outside. In a fever of enthusiasm, Jasmine Herrick offered up a dark-blue blouse with white spots. The white spots were a drawback, but Terry felt one should not look a gift horse in the mouth, and the blue blouse was cut up there and then with someone's nail scissors. There was terrible trouble later on at Jasmine's home, for the blouse was new and the best flannel, but at the moment the Patrol had a comfortable idea that they were 'making do, in a highly creditable manner.'

White blouses were the usual wear at the Manor, and very well they looked with the coloured ties of the different ' Houses.' Jasmine's navy-blue had been an exception, perhaps owing to the fact that she had a habit of spattering ink all over herself when French exercises proved undoable. But not for nothing was Terry a soldier's daughter. "White shows up fearfully," she said "except in snow time, It's almost as bad as red, especially when the sun's shining. Our blouses ought to be some colour like khaki, because in autumn time you can always get a background of that dead-leaf colour, but the book (Guide) says navy blue."

"Awfully nice khaki shirts with a dear little pocket in the blouse at Henry and Dicks'," Birdie suggested. "Of course khaki's a dreadfully ugly colour, but if you think we ought - well the shirts were only eight shillings and eleven pence, each with a duckie little blue piping, and Viyella ones, so they won't get shrunk up and pinch your neck."

Terry, who was sitting on a desk with her legs tucked under her, tailor fashion, nearly slid off in her horror. "Eight shillings and eleven pence each and we've got nineteen shillings and eleven pence to spend on everything!" she said; "besides we don't want blue pipings and fuss, we want something that won't look grubby and horrid directly we start doing things, and listen what we need." She read out solemnly. " Dark blue Guide's hat, felt. We'll each need to have one, for none of our silly hats would look the least like. A pale blue Guide tie. Goodness, what a length! Forty inches, but you use it for signalling and bandaging, and all kinds of things as well as for wearing, so we've jolly well got to have it. Well, tunics or blouses, Patrol emblems and shoulder-knots; skirts, and dark blue knickers under them, we have all got, black stockings too. Then, oh, I say, there's a special brown leather belt with a brass registered Girl-Guide buckle and pouch."

As they have limited funds for uniform they come up with the good idea of using navy 'Dolly Dye' to change the white blouses to navy and to also use blue 'Dolly Dye to dye white silk stockings to wear as ties. Terry can

18

hardly wait however and begins by wearing into lessons her Red-House tie loose with the ends knotted to show that she is a Guide. The other girls in her form do the same with their ties and the poor teacher, Miss Quantock, decides to let them only commenting that "If you are all so anxious for a good deed you may pay proper attention to your writing and spelling." She knew Guides knotted tie ends to remind them to do a good turn.

The girls find it difficult to be Guides with no training available, but this changes after a dangerous incident involving Terry and a mad dog.

Terry is in the village one day with Penelope and they go into the village shop kept by Mr and Mrs Thompson to spend two pence on peppermint rock. While there they are warned that a farm dog behaving 'uncommon queerly' is on the loose and Mr Thompson points out his old service-revolver on the parlour mantelpiece, which he has fetched out in case of trouble with the dog. The girls decide that they will go along to the Infant School, where the children are due out shortly, and give some of their rock to the orphan the Manor School clothes.

"Come on and give the sweets to Bessie, Terry said. Hard on her words came a sound which, once heard, cannot be forgotten, a horrid kind of snarling yelp. Penelope clutched Terry's sleeve. 'What's that?" Both children looked round, and Thompson's story rushed into their minds.

Down the road from the Common it came - a thing that was hardly recognised as Farmer Hayward's mongrel, but usually good-tempered, terrier. It ran in an extraordinary, one-sided way, snapping fiercely at the air as it ran; and every now and again springing right up into the air without any notice of the long chain which hung from its collar and clanked and jangled as its owner jumped and loped along.

Both children stared, dazed for a second. "It's the mad dog," Terry said. Penelope gave a wild tug to her sleeve. "Mrs Simpson's - come inside!" The school clock finished striking. Terry gasped. "The infants! They'll be coming out!" If Terry had ever run in her life she ran then - down the wide sleepy street towards the school which seemed to have grown unaccountably farther away.

"I - run - faster - you - get - inside - Mrs - Simpson's." she threw over her shoulder to Penelope. But Penelope did not go inside; she toiled breathlessly in Terry's wake down the street, hearing that terrible clank and yap and snap behind her, and feeling as though the mad dog were already on her heels. She disobeyed the order boldly, for had not Terry promised her the next good turn?

Terry must have heard her; for she flung another order, which jerked so much that, it was hardly to be heard. "Thompson's service-revolver!" Penelope understood that, and threw herself panting into Mrs Thompson's shop, while Terry continued her headlong race for the school.

Alas! The infants had no intention of staying in an abode of wisdom any longer than they were obliged. They were pouring out, a whole crowd of small things in flapping cotton pinafores. And Terry had no breath to raise a warning shout - the sound that came from between her dry lips was more like a choke, and was drowned in the horrid snapping of the dog as it loped along the street towards the little crowd of children.

Terry swung round - the dog was nearer even than she had thought. She drew a long breath and got out a shriek at last - "Run back to school!" Over her shoulder she could see the children tumbling over each other in their effort to obey the order. They were frightened now, but their fright did not help them to be quick. The dog would get in the middle of them before half could get to cover. And there was no sight of Mr Thompson and the loaded service-revolver.

Terry remembered something that the boys had told her, and pulled out a rather grubby handkerchief. She held it taut between her two hands at arms' length, stood in the middle of the street between the dog and the crying, scrambling children, and waited. The instinct of a dog, whether mad or sane, is to tear down anything in the nature of a stick that bars its path, and then there is a second for the kick under the jaw, which, in this case, must be a disabling one. Terry inwardly doubted the strength of her kick, but somebody must keep the dog off till the infants were safely inside the school again.

The dog was almost on her - Terry saw it crouch to spring, and found herself wishing she were as tall as Tip. And then she was jerked out of the way and somebody had grasped the dog by the back of its neck, and was holding it out at the full length of a left arm. A kind of rocking mist, which had curiously encircled the small girl in that instant when she knew help had come, cleared a little and she saw that her rescuer had only that left arm with which to hold. The empty right sleeve was pinned across his chest. Terry guessed that it was a doubtful question how long he could hold the dog. It writhed as though it had no backbone and made frantic snatches at his face.

"Thompson has a revolver," she said for the second time that afternoon, and the man began running towards the shop, holding out the dog. His hat came off, and Terry saw that his hair and forehead were quite damp. "Cut into the school, kiddie," he said sharply, and as he spoke he all but caught his foot in the trailing chain. Terry deftly snatched it from beneath his feet, feeling the dog fling itself just past her as she did so, and held it up. "I'm a sort of Girl Guide," she gave as a reason and excuse, and ran alongside, holding up the chain. Bursting out of the shop door came Mr Thompson with the service-revolver, followed by Penelope, her spectacles at a rakish angle.

"Close up and through its head!" ordered the one-armed man. "Don't move, Miss Guide!" Terry stood like a rock, and Thompson seized his opportunity. The one-armed man pushed Terry and Penelope into the shop before him. "Thanks; have it cleared away," he said in a low voice to Thompson, and Thompson shifted the smoking service-revolver from the right arm to the left in order to salute with amazing precision and say "Yes, Cap'en."

The one-armed man sat down upon the counter and looked at Terry with an odd expression in his blue eyes. "For only a sort of a Girl-Guide, you seem to have your head screwed on pretty well," he said slowly. "Why only a sort of?"

"We're only Tenderfoots at present." Terry said a little mournfully, "We haven't any one who knows to teach us how to pass our Guide tests, you see.

"If that's all, let us go and ask my old friend, Miss Warwick, to whose school I suppose you belong, if I may put in for the post," he said. "I do happen to know something about tests - I was a Scoutmaster before the War."

Terry then realises that he is Captain Evelyn, V.C. and accepts his kind offer.

He allows them to use a little tower room at his home for their Patrol Headquarters. Many adventures later, with the help of her friends, Terry saves the life of a visitor of Captain Evelyn's after a fire in a laboratory and bravely carries to safety a box of gunpowder which might otherwise have exploded. At supper that night the Head girl, Gytha, 'the great Gytha,' proposes the toast to 'The future Girl-Guides of the Manor.'

Gytha, Terry and the other members of the Lone Patrol are enrolled as Girl-Guides the week after these exciting adventures by the Divisional Commissioner and on the last day of term a big company enrolment is held for 50 girls under the title of '1st Manor Company' with Gytha's sister, now teaching at the school, as Captain.

After the impressive ceremony, which includes Drill, the marching on of the Colours and formation of a Horse-Shoe, each Guide is enrolled by the Commissioner. Each girl marches forward with her Patrol-Leader to take the threefold promise, receive her trefoil badge, shake hands - left-handed of course - and to salute both the Colours and the Company

The Commissioner praises the three Patrol-leaders, Terry Vaughan, Penelope Calcot and Fleur-de-Lys Arden but singles out Terry for special mention:

"Terry Vaughan was faced by a greater opportunity," the Commissioner goes on. "But I want you all to remember that it should be nothing to a Girl Guide whether the opportunity is small or great. 'Do ye nexte thinge' is her motto, whether it is to pick up a piece of banana -skin before people slip on it, or to carry a box of gunpowder out of a room which is on fire. Terry Vaughan rose to receive that royal visitor, Opportunity, but from what I have heard of her I think she hadn't been accustomed to sit still before. It has been decided to award her the Nurse Cavell Badge for special pluck and calmness in danger.

"Company, three cheers for Patrol-leader Terry Vaughan!"

proclaims the Captain.

The big hall, and the crowd of smiling grown-up people, and of wildly cheering Guides, literally goes round with Terry.

The Nurse Cavell Badge, one of the greatest honours a Girl Guide can have! She is only dimly aware that the Commissioner is shaking hands with her. "Go on as you have begun, Guide Terry."

Fact or Fiction?

Becoming Guides in the face of, if not actual opposition but difficulty, is not only the province of fiction. In a real-life Girls' Boarding School, the Abbey School, Malvern Wells, Girl Scouting began there in 1911, only three years after the official start of Boy Scouts and one year after the official start of Girl Guides. The first girls dressed as Scouts had gate-crashed the Boy Scout Rally at the Crystal Palace in 1909, so some girls, particularly those with brothers, were aware of the organisation from the early days.

A pupil in Junior House called Nancy Whatley had returned after school holidays with the newly published 'Scouting for Boys', the book Robert Baden-Powell had written as a manual for Scouts, She had Scout brothers and had seen and read this exciting book. For five years the Abbey Girl Scouts ran themselves under girl Scoutmasters no older than thirteen years of age, all being in the Junior School. The headmistress, Miss Florence Judson, allowed this without interference from the staff and her sister, Miss Alice, took a great interest in them, helping with tents and competitions and saving them from trouble when they became too adventurous. In those early days Girl Scouts would come back from their lunch-break smelling of wood smoke, where they had been practicing fire-lighting and their teacher's reaction can be imagined, also their laundresses must have complained about smoky clothes and the inevitable rips and tears from outdoor activities.

The Troop flourished until Nancy went up to the Senior School at the age of fourteen and things did not go too well then without her natural leadership.

The headmistress sent for a fifth form girl, Olive Hillbrook, who by her own admission had a stormy boarding school career and asked her to be the Scoutmaster of the Junior House Troop. Only after leaving school did Olive discover that this was to use up her excess energy and make her less of a nuisance! She, like Dorothea Moore's fictional Terry, put enormous energy and enthusiasm into this. She even sent her father to the well-known London Store, Gamages, to buy her a uniform, which they certainly would have refused to supply had they known it was for a girl! He also managed to obtain for her Scout badges and enrolment certificates - of course the Scout officials would have been in the dark about their destination.

As the group grew larger in numbers they needed to find an adult to help and Miss Alice agreed to be the official adult - later becoming Commissioner. Under her leadership Scouting developed through the school with the help of the sixth formers.

Scouting continued to flourish as the First World War came to an end and Olive, having left school, returned when possible to help. These enthusiastic Girl Scouts felt they had been safely hidden away in their school by the Malvern Hills and did not want to change from being Scouts to the new Girl Guides, However in 1916 Lady Olave Baden-Powell was visiting St. James's School, West Malvern, another Girls' Boarding School, where Baden-Powell Girl Guides had been officially registered in 1911. She found time to visit the Abbey School and, at a stormy meeting, made a personal appeal for the Scouts to join the official Girl Guide Movement. There were fierce arguments as the girls wanted to keep their individuality, and not to join what they saw as a much tamer body of girls. They were reluctant to lose their Scout hats and staves too but gave in and re-registered as Girl Guides. By giving in they showed great public spirit and one reason for changing was that the larger organisation would give them greater scope for service after leaving school. The school magazines for St. James's School often recorded lists of former pupils and what they were doing in Guiding. Although the school magazines for the Abbey School have not survived the merging of the school with firstly St James's and now Malvern Girls' College they would certainly have recorded the same information about their 'Old Girls.'

Such was the Abbey School's enthusiasm for Guiding that at one time they had five Guide companies, 1st, 2nd, 3rd, 4th and 6th Malvern Wells (Abbey School). When a Guide Company was started in the village of Malvern Wells for local girls it took the title of 5th Malvern Wells.

24

In the early years Guides could have a Cavell badge, a little bronze 'C', if they aimed to grow up to be like the heroine, Nurse Edith Cavell, but this later changed to an Award, the Nurse Cavell Badge, awarded for acts of heroism. Later there were other Guide medals, which could be awarded for gallantry or duty exceptionally well done, these chiefly being the Bronze Cross, the Silver Cross and Medal of Merit.

An early Guide Company – note their solution to uniform!

Chapter 2
The Guide Promise

Perhaps the most important factor distinguishing the Scout and Guide Associations from other youth organisations is the making of a Promise before receiving the enrolment (Promise) badge. The Promise remains central to the programme of each organisation and will be re-affirmed on a number of occasions, at services, camps and after moving from one section of the organisation to another, Someone becoming an adult leader will be called on to re-make their promise, either one to one with a Leader or, if brave enough, in the presence of their Scouts or Guides. Although I use the word Association for Scouts and Guides we more frequently call it a Movement, the idea being that it does move forward with the times to a certain degree as anticipated by the Founder, Lord Baden-Powell.

The original promise for Girl Guides has the wording:

> I promise on my honour to do my best
> To do my duty to God and the King (Queen)
> To help other people at all times
> To obey the Guide Law.

The wording has changed slightly over the years, 'obey' changed to 'keep' and the current wording is:

> I promise that I will do my best:
> To love my God,
> To serve the Queen and my country
> To help other people
> and to keep the Guide Law.

Those of us who made our Promise with the old wording will need to remember the new when called on to renew the Promise, generally at the Thinking Day Service. Thinking Day is celebrated on February 22nd, the joint birthday of Lord and Lady Baden-Powell, the day kept for remembering our fellow Guides and Scouts throughout the world.

Lord Baden-Powell said:
> "Religion seems a very simple thing:
> 1. Love and serve God.
> 2. Love and serve your neighbour."

Before making the Promise there is always discussion on the meaning and how to carry it out in daily life. Even the smallest Rainbow (aged 5 to 7) makes a Promise in a simplified form and the Brownie of today in a near wording, substituting the words 'Brownie Guide Law' for 'Guide Law'. They will understand that the Promise is for every day and every part of life. It is also much the same Promise made by Guides all over the world, in intention if not in actual words.

The early Guides and those today, at the time of their enrolment (Promise Ceremony), share the same intention to make and keep a solemn Promise.

Promises were usually made at a ceremony, in early days to the District or Division Commissioner, later to the Guider, and normally in a formal circle.

Promises today, and for some time, have been a moveable feast, made at camp, on an outing or hike. Some have been made at dawn on a mountaintop, on a climbing wall, up a monument or at a place special to the Guide. The Promise needs to be special for each girl and choosing the place where it is made makes it so.

Muriel Grundy, a Guide in 1ˢᵗ St Barnabas Guide Company. Born 1899, this photo dates from 1916/1917

Chapter 3
The Guide Law

Before making her Promise any member of the Guide Movement is expected to know and to intend to keep the Guide Law. For the early Guides the Law consisted of ten individual laws:

1. A Guide's honour is to be trusted
2. A Guide is loyal
3. A Guide's duty is to be useful and to help others
4. A Guide is a friend to all, and a sister to every other Guide
5. A Guide is courteous
6. A Guide is a friend to animals
7. A Guide obeys orders
8. A Guide smiles and sings under all difficulties
9. A Guide is thrifty
10. A Guide keeps herself pure in thought, word and deed.

The Guide in the early Guide fiction stories would have learned all these and, like my mother and I, used as an aide-memoire the following rhyme -

> Trusty, loyal, helpful,
> Sisterly, courteous, kind,
> Obedient, smiley, thrifty,
> Pure in thought, word and mind!

They might well have giggled at some of this, (but never in front of Captain!), but generally accepted that these laws were possible to live up to.

The wording of these has changed from time to time, to make things clearer or to update an old phrase. Retaining ten laws, they changed to:

1. A Guide is loyal and can be trusted
2. A Guide is helpful
3. A Guide is polite and considerate
4. A Guide is friendly and a sister to all Guides
5. A Guide is kind to animals and respects all living things
6. A Guide is obedient
7. A Guide has courage and is cheerful in all difficulties
8. A Guide makes good use of her time
9. A Guide takes care of her possessions and those of other people
10. A Guide is self-controlled in all she thinks, says and does.

The last change to these Laws, effective from January 1st 1996, abbreviated them to six only:

A Guide is honest, reliable and can be trusted
A Guide is helpful and uses her time and abilities wisely
A Guide faces challenge and learns from her experiences
A Guide is a good friend and a sister to all Guides
A Guide is polite and considerate
A Guide respects all living things and takes care of the world
    around her

Chapter 4

The First Guide Law
'A Guide's honour is to be trusted'

Bunty of the Blackbirds - by Christine Chaundler

Christine Chaundler was born in 1887 in Bedfordshire, one of the large family of Henry Chaundler, a solicitor, and his wife, Henrietta; most of the children died in childhood. Christine wrote when she was a child and spent most of her long life writing books and working in publishing. She died on 15th December 1972 in Sussex.

She wrote many children's stories, some of which were serialised in magazines and was at her peak in the 1920's and 1930's.

This particular book was written in 1925 and published by Nisbet. The Children's Press printed my own edition some time in the 1950's, the dedication being to – Elizabeth Olwen M. Evans, Brynsithin, Dolgelley, Xmas 1952 from A. Cassie.

This story definitely focuses on who can or cannot be trusted, the Guide with the real problems being the well meaning but always in trouble, Bunty Bevan! And haven't we all met her in one guise or another!

The Blackbird Patrol, including Petronella Mayne, known as Peter, Theo Burton, Eileen Draycott and Mary Wild, are found in the class 4A sitting room at school a week before the end of the summer term. There are five Guide Patrols in Moxton House School Guides and they are looking forward to going to camp and to the Patrol Competition, won by the

Blackbirds last year.

Joan, Peter's cousin, their Patrol Second, has had to accompany a sick aunt to Switzerland, leaving a vacancy for a Second in the Patrol. They think that Peter may be chosen to fill it by the Patrol Leader, Sheila. As there is also the spare place in their Patrol, they are wondering who will come along. However the Guiders have been overheard saying that they will need to form a second School Guide Company, and will leave the Patrols as they are for camp.

The Blackbirds are glad that they haven't been given either a Tenderfoot, or Bunty Bevan, correctly Bunty Rosemary Marcella Bevan, who is in their Class. While she is willing and honest, she is always 'putting her foot in it' and is clumsy and always in trouble, although always well meaning. Her parents have decided not to let her go to camp this year.

Bunty bursts in, causing her usual chaos, to tell them that she can go to camp after all, and their Guide Captain, Miss Benson, has said she will let her, provided she passes her Second Class test. She is determined to do it!

Her Guide friends looked at one another in dismay:

It was awfully jolly for Bunty, of course, but – but it was going to be very rough luck on whichever Patrol it was that she was drafted into. Bunty was such a hopeless person over her Guide work that perhaps it wasn't altogether surprising that just for a moment some of her fellow-Guides almost forgot the spirit of the Fourth Guide Law which Miss Benson, their Captain, tried so hard to make them understand.

Bunty, not usually very quick to notice things, sees their faces and asks if they aren't glad she will be going to camp. The girls deny this and make her welcome, and agree that they will help her. She thinks they are all bricks and Peter offers to help her with her knots in the half hour before tea. Aiming to find a cord and be helpful, Bunty nearly demolishes a hanging blind, but admits she is in the wrong and offers to report it to Matron. Although some of the others disagree, she fears one of the maids may get the blame and goes to report herself.

After she leaves the girls discuss the news that she will be camping and decide that it is quite likely she will be 'dumped' on them. This will mean they will lose their chance of being Star Patrol at camp, but they agree they will not hurt her by letting her know that they are not pleased to have her.

The last week of term goes by quickly and they help Bunty with her Guide Morse and with knotting. They know that all she has left to do is to light a fire in the open with just two matches and, in their enthusiasm to help her, decide to help her to do this without asking permission. Peter, Mary, Eileen and Bunty discuss this:

"Peter, don't you think we could get permission so that she could practise really lighting it? I believe Miss Benson would let us if we asked."

"She might," said Peter. "On the other hand, she mightn't! If we asked and she said 'No', it would be awkward, for we couldn't very well do it then. I think we'd be wiser not to ask."

"We can't just do it without asking though, can we?" Bunty said.

"Just depends," said Peter, with a mischievous twinkle in her eyes. "If we could get hold of a box of matches, and could manage to slip away somewhere on the q.t., I don't see why it mightn't be done."

They decide there will be no problem in getting the matches from a new maid and they will break rules by slipping away from the Saturday school cricket match to go on the Common to practise lighting a fire.

They decide how and when they can slip away unnoticed but Bunty is not so keen, being afraid that somehow she will mess up their plans, but they manage to persuade her.

They hope to have two hours to do this and to have a picnic, so assemble the necessary equipment, taking some of it to hide by the Lodge. They go to the match concealing other things they need on their persons or under the rugs they take to sit upon. They sit by a gap in the hedge and wait for Bunty, who arrives late, her suspender having broken, and one of the teachers has made her sew it back on with cotton. Luckily she isn't carrying anything to arouse suspicion and, when the batsmen are running for four and other onlookers' attention is taken, the guides manage to slip through the gap undetected. They have to cross two fields, fences, and then scramble down a grassy bank into a lane, which leads them to the Common. Having found a sheltered spot Theo and Eileen go off to find water, while Bunty, supervised by Peter, lays her fire, Peter waiting for a whistled signal to say water has been found. She can then take the dixie (cooking pot) to carry the water.

When the signal is heard she leaves Bunty to light the fire ready to boil the water, which Bunty is trying to do when she hears voices. There are two men talking about a 'job' they are on, which will enable them to be well off. They use betting terms and Bunty thinks that is what they are discussing.

As soon as they have moved a safe distance away along the track she looks out and sees that there is one short man and a tall man with a limp, both scruffy, and she dismisses them from her mind as tramps or poachers. Emerging from her hiding place she is horrified to see that the match she has discarded, (and thought was extinguished), has set fire to a gorse bush and a patch of the Common. She tries to beat it out with a big stick, but only succeeds in setting the skirt of her short gym tunic alight. Fortunately the rest of the Patrol return and Peter and Theo between them fling the water Peter is carrying over Bunty's skirt and throw her to the ground to put out the fire.

As the material is thick it has burned only slowly and little harm done, and the other Guides attack the burning gorse, putting the fire out.

They are quite cross with Bunty and there is no time left to go back for more water or to boil it for tea. Bunty apologises and looks very unhappy:

"All right, kid. Don't look so scared. It wasn't your fault so much as your misfortune," Peter said kindly.

Bunty is very shaken and, as they have no water to give her to drink, they give her some of the watermelon they have brought for their picnic. As she begins to look better they sit down to eat their picnic and she tells them what has distracted her, hearing the two men and her feeling they were up to no good. They then turn their attention to how they can smuggle Bunty back into school without anyone in authority spotting the tremendous hole burnt into her gym tunic.

"We must get her in without anybody knowing somehow. It's going to mean the most ghastly row for us if we don't," Peter said.

"An absolutely appalling row," Theo agreed grimly.

"I say, you – you don't think it will mean our being stopped going to camp, do you?" Eileen asked in sudden alarm.

Nobody answered her for a moment. Then Theo said reluctantly: "Don't know. Wish I was sure that it wouldn't!"

"Unluckily it will be a Guide row," Peter said, with a worried frown. "It didn't seem a very dreadful thing to do when we were planning it – just to break bounds for one afternoon to help Bunty pass her test. But now – well, I don't know what you others think, but – but, I must say, I'm a bit scared now."

The faces of the others show very clearly what they think. As Peter has said, it hasn't seemed a very dreadful thing to do as long as it appears to be a perfectly safe thing. Bunty's misfortune has put a very different aspect on the whole affair. Now, instead of being perfectly safe, it appears that discovery is extremely probable, and the crime seems to grow in enormity every moment to the guilty consciences of the five.

"I know what Miss Benson would say. She'd say that if our honour isn't to be trusted in term-time, she wouldn't be able to trust it in camp," Mary says.

Bunty again apologises and suggests that they go back as planned and she will slip in through the kitchen garden and try to reach the dorm without being caught. She can then put on her other tunic and hide the burnt one and feels it will be easier for her to get in on her own, and if she is caught it will be only herself, not the Blackbird Patrol who will be stopped from going to camp or get in a row.

Peter says that if she is caught, they will all, of course, own up:

"Nice sort of Guides we'd be if we didn't!"

Peter goes with Bunty and manages to smuggle her into the school grounds and, climbing on a wooden box, into the boot lobbies. They reach the corridor leading to the dormitory, but Matron catches Peter, who says that she has cut her finger and has come to find a hanky. Bunty has hidden and reaches her dormitory, kneeling to find her spare tunic and knickers, but is caught by Miss Benson, who is, of course, the School Guide Captain. Miss Benson is looking for Matron but now sees the burnt clothes and asks for an explanation.

Bunty, after a few attempts to conceal what has happened, has to tell Miss Benson that she has been trying to practise making a fire outdoors for her Tenderfoot, setting herself alight! She keeps the other Guides out of the explanation.

Miss Benson is genuinely shocked at the narrow escape Bunty has had:

> She made no further enquiries as to the culprit's accomplices or lack of accomplices, but, taking it for granted, apparently, that she had none, she proceeded to read her a lecture upon Guide ideals and a Guide's sense of honour, pointing out how dreadfully she had failed to live up to the one and how grievously she had transgressed against the other. And Bunty stood and listened in dumb misery, conscious of the enormity of the crime, though it is to be feared not very clear as to wherein she had sinned the most – in breaking bounds to practise fire-lighting, or in her carelessness in setting herself alight and bringing about discovery.
>
> "I can't tell you how grieved I am to think that one of my Guides could have done such a thing," said Miss Benson.

Bunty apologises and Miss Benson' anger melts away, as she sees how sorry she is, but when Bunty asks if this means she will not be able to camp, Miss Benson has to decide how to deal with her. She decides that she will not report Bunty to the Head, if she will give her word of honour that she will not do such a thing again. She will hold a Court of Honour on the next Monday to decide about camp:

> "I am sorry to leave you in suspense for such a long time, but it cannot be helped. If, as I hope, the Court of Honour should be willing to give you another chance to prove yourself trustworthy, you will have to look upon the uncertainty now as part of your punishment."

Bunty accepts this, but is awestricken as the Court of Honour is a committee formed of the officers and the patrol leaders of the company to consider important matters relating to the Guides. She asks if Peter and the other Blackbirds may not be told about this, as they have been helping her to pass her test in case she is made a Blackbird.

Round Table Conference.

Ranger Round Table similar to a Court of Honour. Pen drawing from a logbook.

Miss Benson agrees, but wonders if the others have been goading Bunty to pass her test until she has lost her sense of right and wrong in her anxiety to please them. Bunty now has to keep the Blackbirds from hearing that she has been caught and the Captain and patrol leaders from guessing that the Blackbirds have been involved. She wants to keep her friends out of trouble:

> Once let the others get any inkling of what had happened up in the dormitory, and they would feel obliged, as in honour bound, to go and give them selves up to justice, too.

She is very afraid, that if the others' part in the escapade comes to light, they will not be allowed to go to camp:

> No! There was only one thing to be done. Somehow or other every one must be prevented from learning the facts of the case. And though Bunty hadn't the faintest idea of how she was going to see

the business through, she had made up her mind that somehow or other she would do it:

"It's my fault for being such an idiot. It's only fair that I should take the blame," Bunty thought, as she made her way into the dining-hall for tea.

Bunty tells the others that she has managed to reach her cubicle safely, which is a relief to her friends. They hear of the Court of Honour, to be held after the weekend as the second Guide officer, Miss Kerr, is away, but do not associate this with their ill doings. They do wonder why Bunty has been summoned, but after the Court of Honour, which none of them, of course, attend, accept her explanation that she has been told that she may not try for her Second Class before camp. They don't think that this is fair but have to accept the decision.

Miss Benson's actual words to Bunty are:

"After your escapade on Saturday, Bunty, we do not feel that we can give you your Second Class Badge just now. We are not satisfied that you have as yet quite grasped the spirit of the Guide Law, and we would rather wait until we feel that we can trust your honour again."

The Blackbirds know that Bunty has not been drafted into any Patrol yet, but is still in the 'Recruits Squad' – invented by Miss Benson for new Guides until they know the basics of Guiding. They know Bunty has always been an unsatisfactory Guide and has been left in this squad, so are not as surprised as they might have been at the Court of Honour's decision. They try to be cheerful about having to take Bunty to camp in their Patrol and Peter says they will help her to be a satisfactory Guide and have her Second Class badge in camp.

They go to camp, with Bunty still keeping her secret, although the Patrol Leader of the Blackbirds, now Moira Neil, knows but doesn't tell the others. Peter has been chosen as Second and Bunty has been put into the vacant space. The patrol help Bunty prepare for camp and arrive at the site to pitch their tent. They had full marks for this last year and Peter is at pains to tell Bunty not to do anything on her own, but to help the others. Trying to clear thistles from the ground where they are pitching, Bunty cuts her hand, nearly fainting and has to be carried to the First Aid tent by the others, where Miss Lester, the First Aider, deals with the cut. Moira is kind to Bunty and the others soon pitch the tent, but the Blackbirds come bottom in the tent-pitching contest. They are not too down hearted as they are at camp for a fortnight and they will be able to catch up.

Guides clearing a field for camping, removing bracken.

However, when they are Water Patrol, Bunty again is in trouble as she cannot do heavy work with a bandaged hand, but is left to tie tapes on the handles of the buckets – red for washing-water and white for drinking water. Bunty is worrying about having forgotten her toothbrush and that she may lose marks for the Patrol, as a record is being kept at camp as in school of teeth being cleaned each day! Worrying, she does not concentrate on the job in hand and cannot decide if it is worse to tell her Patrol Leader now or wait until bedtime. She finds out from a Guide in the Robin Patrol that the village is not too far away, and wonders if she can get permission to go there to buy something. The reply is that the shops are shut now but that they have been doing the shopping and could have got whatever she wants, had they known earlier.

Told that Bunty needs to buy a toothbrush, the Robin says that chemists usually keep open later than other shops, but Dorothy Harding has asked for permission to go to buy a comb and been refused. Captain has given her a bad mark and told her to wait until morning, so she suggests that Bunty lies low and says nothing and hopes that her Leader will forget to hand the book round on the first night.

Bunty doesn't think Moira will let anyone overlook cleaning her teeth and is now sure she will get a bad mark if she asks to go to the village. She decides to risk it and slips off to the village using a short cut over the moor. No one sees her go and she very soon is lost with dusk falling. She tries to be brave, but then hears people approaching, quarrelling as they come. She asks them the way to the Guides' Camp, which is in Lord Rosmere's meadow, and the mention of this name seems to rouse the suspicions of one of the men. The other however gives her directions, although he says he is a stranger. She is glad to get away from them, realising that they may have been the two men on Moxton Common on the day of the fire.

Very afraid that the Blackbirds will lose points for this latest escapade, she is on her way back to camp when she meets the rest of the Blackbird Patrol, who have been searching for her. In fact they have made enquiries in the village and practically the whole company has been out searching. Miss Benson is very cross:

"I really do not know what to say to you, Bunty," Miss Benson said in grave reproach when she had extracted the story of the quest for the toothbrush. "I am growing very sorry that I ever brought you to camp. You seem to have only the most rudimentary idea of the meaning of the promise you made when you were enrolled as a Guide. You promised to obey the Guide Law. What is the first article of that Law, can you tell me?"

"A- a Guide's Honour is to be trusted," murmured Bunty in a choked little voice.

"And how have you obeyed? I am beginning to fear that I shall never be able to trust your honour. Don't you realise what a very dishonourable thing it was to steal out of camp in that underhand way?"

Bunty nodded miserably.

"Yes, only – only I was afraid of getting a bad mark for forgetting my toothbrush and losing points for the Patrol," she said.

Miss Benson tells her that she has made it worse for her Patrol, who will lose even more points. She sends her to have supper before bed and will deal with her in the morning. She also tells Bunty that Miss Lester will give her a toothbrush as she always brings spares, and Bunty realises it has all been for nothing.

Her Patrol Leader scolds her and they do lose a lot of points, not just for the toothbrush incident, but also because when they were Water Patrol the night before there had been a mix up with the buckets. Some of the water from the spring, not to be used for drinking, had been put in buckets with no red tapes on, but they had white tapes on, showing the water was for drinking. Luckily the mistake was discovered before anyone had drunk the impure water, but the Patrol responsible would have no points for the work. Bunty knows it is her fault and pleads with Miss Benson that it is not the Blackbird Patrol's fault, but Miss Benson says that although she is sorry for the Blackbirds for having such an unsatisfactory Guide in their Patrol, this cannot be helped. The whole Patrol has to be responsible. It has been decided to punish Bunty for running off by confining her to bounds for two days, which Bunty doesn't mind as long as the Patrol are not losing more points!

Guides in the Water Patrol at Camp at Borth in August 1932.

Camp progresses with the Guiders carefully keeping an eye on Bunty and not letting her do very much. She notices a very small boy come into the camp, with a nursemaid following him, and takes his hand to take him to his nurse. He likes the guides who he calls 'soldier-girls', but runs off, chased by Bunty and the nurse, and only quick action by the Robin Patrol Leader prevents him from running into the kitchen fire. He is David, Lord Rosmere's son, and has run off while his nurse has been picking flowers for her mistress. By now the child is kicking and screaming and she is grateful to them for helping her catch him and saving him from the fire. He is the apple of his father's eye.

She takes him home, although he is still calling to the girls.

The Blackbird Patrol do not blame Bunty for letting David escape her, but envy the Robins for their Patrol Leader's quick action, and because they are getting so awfully far ahead in the competition. They keep watch over Bunty when she helps with chores, having been told by their Patrol leader, Moira, that Miss Benson is concerned they may have been 'not quite kind to their Tenderfoot member.' Bunty again apologises to them for her actions and feels they are being 'jolly decent.'

Although the Patrol has worked hard in camp, by the end of the first week they are still several points behind the other Patrols:

"Only another week to catch up in, too!" sighed Peter. "I don't believe we've got an earthly chance of doing it unless a miracle occurs. We shall come out bottom of the camp competition this year, I'm afraid. It will be a fearful come-down for us after being top."

She hadn't meant Bunty to hear that, and had waited to say it until Bunty had gone out of the tent, where they were all getting ready for bed, on her way to the washing cubicles. But Bunty had dropped her sponges just outside and had stopped to pick them up, and had overheard every word of it, and she went away wishing more fervently than ever that somehow, someway, somewhere, she could make herself a better Guide.

Lord Rosmere arrives at the camp during rest hour and the Guides think he has come to thank Rose, the Robin Patrol Leader, who has saved his son, David, from the fire. However, after he has spoken to Captain, the Patrol Leaders are called over and told that his son has disappeared, and Lord Rosmere has come to see if they have seen him. He is starting search parties and Miss Benson has offered to let the Guides all go to search too. This is passed on to the Patrols who get ready very quickly, and Lord Rosmere thanks them for offering to help and says he will thank them some other time for their previous help.

The Guides know the area quite well now and the Patrols go in various directions, but have no success and return to camp for six fifteen, Miss

Benson going up to Lord Rosemere's house to report their failure. When she returns she tells them that David has not been found.

Bunty thinks it over, being rebuked by her Leader for her absentmindedness, and has a startling idea. She does not sleep well, thinking over her idea, but decides as she dresses that she will keep this to herself in case the others laugh at her.

Miss Benson calls at Rosmere House early and there has been no news of the boy, but Moira and Rose, who have been with her, tell the Guides more about how the child has wandered off. Even the bloodhounds have not found his trail further than the shrubbery. The Guides are keen to go out to search again and Miss Benson decides to let them, sending them out with sandwiches for an all-day hike. Miss Kerr stays in camp with four girls, who are not too well, and the Patrols go out separate ways. Bunty tells Peter about her idea, which is about the two men she has seen on the afternoon of the fire at Moxton Common and again in the woods here, when she was going to the village for the toothbrush. She wonders if they have anything to do with the child's disappearance. Peter asks her to repeat all she heard them say and Bunty remembers how one of the men had been angry when she had asked the way:

'and said that if I came from Rosmere's place, I could get back to it. He called me a spying little devil.'

Peter thinks there may be something in this and wants to tell Moira, but can't, as she will have to tell her about the picnic too. She decides to tell the rest of the Patrol without Moira present but finds it difficult to find an opportunity until after tea, when the Leaders have gone to a Court of Honour.

They all want to tell Moira, but agree that as a Prefect she will have to tell Miss Benson everything. Bunty offers to tell her just about her part, but the others decide they will follow up the lead themselves. They plan to slip out at night when Moira is sound asleep and to be back in time for normal camp rising.

They manage to leave at eleven and it is easy walking as the moon is shining and make their way to the place in the woods where they had found Bunty, leaving a trail behind them to help them go back. They then go to where Bunty met the two men - a boggy spot, and as they go they find clues – the remains of a campfire and a can, which has held corned beef, and some sweets. The sweets are in a bag from Pilchard's, a sweetshop in Moxton, so they are sure the two men are the men seen by Bunty on Moxton Common. They must have kidnapped the child enticing him with sweets. As they think they have plenty of time they follow the paths onto a track, but feeling tired they rest and fall asleep! They sleep until four fifteen and decide to go back to camp, taking the corned beef tin and the sweets with them. Peter shakes the tin and finds a little white kid shoe inside, so they know they are right. She sensibly decides that this is now beyond them and sends a Guide back to tell Miss Benson what they have discovered. They decide that the best Guides should go on and Bunty volunteers to go back, so Peter gives her the clues and tells her to tell Miss Benson everything, waking Moira first to go with her.

Bunty makes her way towards camp, feeling quaky and unhappy and wishing they had all stayed together. She goes on becoming increasingly weary and so does not go warily, 'with eyes and ears alert for what might be ahead, as, of course, any Guide worth her salt should have done.'

She comes to the clearing where they had found the paper bag of sweets and the two men are there, the short stocky little man with a sack over his shoulder, watching the tall thin man with the limp, who is hunting about in the undergrowth – the two men the rest of the Blackbirds are searching for.

She gives a startled cry and the men see her, the tall man being cross with her and grabbing her by the wrist, accusing her of spying. She denies this and says she is trying to get back to camp. The short man tries to convince her they are only woodcutters, looking for rabbits and Bunty half believes him, but then the tall man threatens her that, if she tells on them, they will throw her down a quarry nearby. Bunty knows now that they are up to no good, and just then the sack on the small man's shoulders moves and she hears a cry from it, so she pulls away and runs off to hide.

She overhears their conversation, which proves they have kidnapped the child, who is in the sack! She also hears that they are waiting for someone to fetch them and the child in a car at seven o'clock. Bunty knows that this is an hour away and is afraid for the boy, cramped in the sack and crying and thinks what she can do. She stalks them to the road, where they sit down to wait, and pull the child out of the sack. Bunty is full of pity for the frightened child, gagged with a hanky, and, when they remove the gag, he cries for his mother. The man called Jake tries to get him to eat, but he will not. Bunty hears the sound of a car horn and she doesn't want the men to escape with the child, but then sees four blue-clad figures coming down the hillside, so she calls Peter and running over, picks him up and runs towards her friends. When the men realise what is happening they chase her and she puts the child down and tells him to run to the girls. The short man looks on in horror as he knows that the child is running towards the disused quarry, only then does Bunty realise she has sent him into danger. She reaches the quarry and looks down at the black pool of water in the bottom and spots the child coming to the surface. Throwing off her hat, haversack and shoes, she bravely plunges into the pool to save the child.

The two kidnappers save her and the child and the third man, the driver, takes them to Lord Rosmere's house, the men are then arrested.

Bunty is the heroine of the hour and is looked after at Rosmere House, to which her friends come. Peter now knows that Bunty has kept from them the fact that she has been punished over the fire incident, and Theo tells her that she is now to be allowed to try for her Second Class. She is also being recommended to Headquarters for the Bronze Cross. Moira now says that Bunty is the most distinguished member of the company, let alone the patrol. They are meant to keep this a secret and Bunty can hardly believe it. Peter tells her she is a credit to the company and teases her gently and they tell her the whole story of the rescue and that the kidnappers had rescued her and the child. Lord Rosmere is to find jobs for them and the car driver when they finish their prison sentences.

Bunty asks Peter if she really means that she is a credit to the company and not a disgrace:

"I've lost you the camp competition, you know; you'll never be able to catch up with the

Early Guide Award

Robins now. You – you weren't pulling my leg?"

"Pulling your leg? As if I should, over a thing like that. What do you take me for? Who cares if we lose the camp competition or not now, I should like to know? The Robins can win the most points if they like - silly swankers! - but it won't make the remotest difference. Every Guide in the company knows now that the Blackbirds are the smartest Patrol whatever they may do in the competition. And it's all owing to you, Bunty."

Fact or Fiction?

This is a good story to illustrate the first Guide Law, as there are many direct references to it and in situations where it is easy to explain. Bunty is a Guide familiar to most generations of Guides, the enthusiastic but careless girl who is liked by everyone, but a complete disaster to have in your Patrol! I am sure this was as true in the 1920's as today.

If we are honest ourselves we can remember not wanting someone in our Patrol or in our tent at camp. I certainly can. Bunty in this story tries hard to be trustworthy and desperately wants not to let her Patrol down. She needs their trust as much as her Guide Captain's, but, although they try hard to help her, she often lets them down and at camp, loses them points!

This Law was justifiably the First Guide Law, and, as Baden-Powell explained, to say this is the same as taking a solemn oath. If you are trusted to do something, then you do it as well as you can and are not deflected from doing this. Other breaches of trust would be telling a lie or not carrying out an order when trusted to do so.

Those early Guides lived for the most part in an ordered society, where rules did apply, not only the Laws of the land, but there were rules in schools, churches, homes and not surprisingly in your Guide Company Meetings.

You would be trusted to abide by these and if not would then expect to be in some sort of trouble.

Guides at a Company Meeting would be expected to be worthy of trust and could be allowed to go on a hike and clear up after themselves, to follow a clear order from someone in authority, Patrol Leader or Guide Captain.

In this story it takes some time before Bunty can be trusted to do something without close supervision, and also, on more than one occasion, she is the cause of the other members of the Patrol also breaking rules. The Guides know they are not allowed to slip away from watching the Cricket match to go on the Common to light a fire, even if they are helping Bunty to pass a test. However they do it and when things go wrong, Bunty setting fire to the gorse, then her skirt, they are quite prepared to cover this up. Only the conscience stricken Bunty owns up when caught and is prepared to take the punishment herself and not to tell on the others. They have all on this occasion shown they cannot be trusted.

Some of the incidents in this book are almost unbelievable to our modern eyes; take for example the possible mix up with the safe and unsafe water. We would not be allowed to camp now without a safe supply for all purposes, but I have letters from Guides of the 1920's describing the chains of Guides they formed to draw water from the river in buckets.

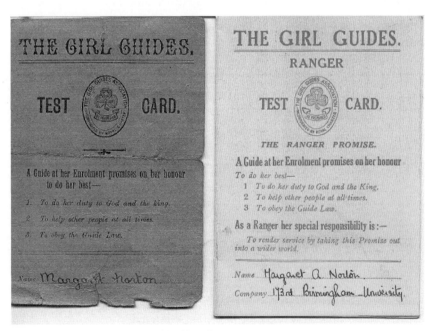

1930's Test Cards. Margaret Norton.

Fetching water in buckets has always been a normal chore at camp, and oh, how lovely it is to just turn on a tap when you come home!

We lay less emphasis now in Guiding on passing Badge Tests, but this book shows very clearly the importance placed on completing first the Tenderfoot Test and then the Second Class badge. This is reflected for me in the number of Test Cards we have in the Archives, kept as treasured personal possessions.

A Patrol of 5th Malvern Wells Guides in the 1930's with my mother, Eva George, their Lieutenant, standing behind them, outside the Tin Hut, where they met.

The Courts of Honour mentioned in this book were certainly still held in my Guide Company in the 1950's, and I have no doubt that in the early days this was a democratic way of self-governing and its findings were important to the running of a Guide Company. I do not recall ever being at one deciding on a Guide's future, but certainly remember, as a Prefect at school, being called on, at a Prefect's meeting, to decide on a punishment for someone breaking school rules (sometimes for smoking in the toilets at break!). The offender was called before the Meeting to be told their punishment. I do not believe this could happen today, but the Guide Court of Honour in the story deals fairly with Bunty and she accepts both its right to decide and its decision.

At the end of the story Bunty has become a heroine for her rescue of a child from drowning and is to be recommended to Guide Headquarters for a Bronze Cross Award for Gallantry. She has become a heroine and her Company and Patrol are proud of her. Hopefully she will keep the 1st Guide Law thereafter!

Later on, in the Second World War, Guides were trusted in many situations, helping with evacuees and at rest centres, and in some cases running messages for the Home Guard. Funds were raised for many different projects, giving service. Older girls helped in children's homes and in fruit-picking camps and some Sea Rangers on the Thames in London. After the War the Guide International Service sent teams of Guiders, along with other organisations, into the occupied countries to help.

Guides continue to be seen as trustworthy and this Law still is at the heart of Guiding.

Chapter 5

The Second Guide Law
'A Guide is loyal'

'The Marigolds Make Good' - by Catherine Christian

Catherine Christian was very involved with Guiding throughout her life, in fact from the 1920's. She was born in 1901 in London, the only child of parents of German origin, later adopting an English surname.

She ran various Guide companies and during the Second World War shared a flat in Battersea with a friend, Margaret Tennyson, a niece of Alfred Lord Tennyson. They both worked at Guide Headquarters in Buckingham Palace Road editing the magazines 'The Guide' and 'The Guider'. When their flat was blitzed they lived for a time in a gipsy caravan, firstly in Sussex and then in Woldingham in Surrey, where they started a Guide Company with Margaret as Captain and Catherine as Lieutenant.

Towards the end of the War she was involved with the Guide International Service.

Her book, 'The Big Test', telling the story of the Girl Guides in the Second World War, remains the best reference material for the activities of the Guide Organisation at that time.

After the War she lived in South Devon, at one time helping a friend with a home for war orphans, and died in 1985.

She wrote many books, Guiding and schoolgirls stories, children's books and adult novels.

For anyone living through either the First or Second World Wars loyalty to one's country was a familiar concept. This novel was written in 1937, when to Guides and those who ran Guiding, making and keeping the Guide laws was a solemn undertaking. In 'The Marigolds Make Good' the loyalty involved is to a Guide Patrol and to Guiding.

Dust wrapper is correct for the bright blue 1950's uniform and the reprinted book. In the original uniform would have been the earlier navy.

The story begins with St Bridget's School having a new Headmistress, Miss Nesbitt, once a pupil herself. The previous Headmistress, Miss Wilson, had founded the school and after fifty years' service retired in failing health.

The school has grown slack and Miss Nesbitt decides to close all School clubs and societies, hoping to improve results in schoolwork and sports. This includes the Guide Company, which now has twenty members only out of three hundred pupils. She intends to review this in September when the new school buildings open.

The Marigold Patrol, led by Norah and mainly made up of red-headed girls decide to continue as a Patrol:

"Miss Blagrove, their captain, had christened them "The Marigold Patrol" the first time she saw their red heads all in a line. They had accepted the title joyfully, and been on the look out, ever since, for red-headed recruits.

But none had appeared, until Mary Glover, small and shy and short-sighted, came as a new girl into Biddie Ormonde's form at St. Bridget's and unexpectedly announced she would like to join the Guides."

They agree that they have only been playing at Guides before and that their Captain has let them off things and accepted excuses from them, trying to make the work part of Guiding easy for them. They plan to prove that they are proper Guides:

" We could try!" Norah turned and her face was suddenly very grave. There just isn't anything we can't have a good shot at, if we stick together and really work. Listen to me, all of you – it's such a waste to play about and pretend to be Guides, when we can perfectly well start from today to *be* Guides, I don't want to make good for what we can get out of it – as a sort of bribe for Miss Nesbitt to let us have a company again. I want to do it as an experiment, for the fun and the adventure."

Mary Glover, a small eleven year old, comes to see Norah to find out if it is true that the Guide Company is to close and Norah confirms that it is to be announced on Monday morning. Mary says:

"Captain told me. I went round to her house last night to tell her Mother couldn't afford my uniform yet, and she told me that the head-mistress was s'pending Guides until further notice. But I don't see how you can s'pend Guides, really, do you?"

Norah looked at the solemn little face curiously.

"How do you mean, Mary? We aren't to have any more meetings until September – perhaps not then."

"Yes, but meetings aren't Guides," Mary persisted cheerfully. "Not any more than uniform is. Uniform's nice, and so are meetings, but they aren't the 'sential parts of Guiding, are they?"

Decidedly taken aback, Norah stared at her recruit.

"Now who taught you that, I wonder?" she meditated. "It's what I've been saying out loud for about three years, but I doubt if even Patsy has taken it in, so far. Where did you get the hang of things from, young Mary?"

"Chief Scout," said Mary promptly. "I've read every one of his books. I'd read a lot before I came here, and I found the rest in the Junior Public Library. Then, of course, I had Mother's *How Girls Can Help to Build the Empire*. I read that when I was seven, and I've played at bits out of it ever since."

"Was your mother a Guide, then?" Norah asked. Mary nodded.

"Yes," she added conscientiously, "She still is of course. She says you can't stop being, once you've been enrolled. You can be a bad Guide, or a good Guide – because you do promise for always, don't you?"

"You do," Norah agreed.

Although the Guide Captain has suggested she might join another company in Oakleigh, Mary wants to remain with the Marigolds. She checks that they will go on being a Patrol and says that Captain thought they might.

Mary is from a poorer background than the others in the Patrol and has come to school on a scholarship, The Marigolds agree that she will have more fun with them than in another company and they will teach her things so that she can be enrolled when the company starts again.

They decide to learn about herbs and trails from a local Gipsy called Ellie and walk through Lady Royston's woods to see her. Arriving at her dilapidated hut they find two estate workers trying to move her against her wishes and they decide to go to see Lady Royston to stop this. They meet Lady Royston when they help her to get her pigs back into their pigsties from in her garden. She takes them into her house and learns that they are Guides.

She agrees not to make Ellie move and that there has been a misunderstanding.

She gives them tea and tells them a little about her childhood and that she was at the original Guide Association's Training School.

MEETING LADY ROYSTON!
Page 43   *Frontispiece*

Lady Royston and her pigs.

52

Afterwards she was a Commissioner and, although she has given up Guiding after spending years in Hungary with her daughter, she hasn't forgotten all about it:

Biddie bent forward, and stared at her earnestly.

"Do you think it was fair of Miss Nesbitt to suspend our company?" she asked.

Lady Royston ignored the murmur of expostulation from Norah and Pat, as she said cheerfully: " Fair or not fair, it needn't do you much harm unless you let it. Tell me more about your plans for 'making bad.'

"Well, as a matter of fact," Norah owned, " we haven't got many yet. We meant to have a Patrol Council this afternoon, but –" she spread out her hands expressively.

"What with rescuing gipsies and hunting baby pigs there hasn't been a lot of time," Lady Royston ended the sentence for her. "Well, now – what do you want to do? Scatter tin tacks in a car park, or burgle the Bank of England, or what?"

"Oh, no!" Norah's face crinkled into delighted denial. " We don't want to do those sort of bad things at all. We want to be Guides just as much as ever. You know, help other people at all times and that sort of thing. But we want to make an adventure of it, instead of being dull and stodgy and goody-goody."

Hearing that they are looking for real 'Good Turns' to do, she challenges them to make a proper home for Ellie before the winter comes. She also invites them to visit her any Saturday afternoon so that she can instruct them in Guide subjects.

The girls decide to find out all they can about building a house, so that they can help Ellie, and two of them plan to look at a new house being built on Ringan's estate. Walking there Norah and Biddie decide to help Ellie to grow her own herbs in a garden round her house. They can then help her to sell them and make her own living.

They find a carpenter, Jim, working on the house and chat to him, asking about how houses are built, but are interrupted by the builder, Mr Hewlett, who orders them off the site. He feels they are wasting the men's time. They explain that they are Guides, but that makes no difference to him.

They decide to meet another of the Guides from school and walk down the long hill into the town, noticing that the traffic signals are not working properly. This causes an accident involving an old two-seater car and a schoolboy on a bike. The boy has a small girl up in front of him, clutching the handles and as the bike falls over the child is thrown off into the path of the main road traffic. Norah saves the child from being hit by a sports car and deals with the minor grazes, sending the child home with the boy. She has injured her elbow on the car mudguard and doesn't want a fuss made, but Biddie, with a doctor father, examines the arm and says it is not broken.

The driver of the two-seater is Mr Hewlett, who is very impressed with Norah's behaviour and takes her to sit in his car while Biddie finishes off a bandage on Norah's arm. He listens to their reason for going to his building site and agrees to help them.

The girls visit Ellie, the gipsy, and she treats Norah's injured arm with herbs and they tell her that they plan to build her a new home. She agrees to teach them about plants and herbs and also birds and animals.

When they visit Lady Royston she sets them challenges and they have enormous fun.

Mr Hewlett tells them about framed huts, like the Army has used:

"That sounds marvellous," Norah said enthusiastically. "I say, Mr Hewlett, perhaps if we got a hut like that for Ellie we could put it together ourselves?"

"Not knowing what you young ladies could do if you tried!" he chuckled. Then he grew serious. " You could do a tidy part of the work yourselves, Miss, that I tell you straight – or I daresay one or two of the chaps who work with me'd give a hand, in the evenings, with the heavy part of the job, just for the lark of the thing – that young Jimmie Willox now – he is a Scout – spends his Saturday running around in short trousers, with a pack of little nippers 'e calls 'cubs', we'll make him do his day's good deed, when the time comes and no mistake!"

They are taken aback by the cost of the framed hut, even though Mr Hewlett can have it delivered free of charge to the local railway station and will fetch it himself from there. They are not daunted however and plan to raise the money needed. Mr Hewlett helps by offering them the chance to do some carpentry for profit and will lend them tools.

On the Marigold Patrol's next visit to Lady Royston they meet her niece, Andrea, who isn't able to be a Guide herself, as her father's job in the diplomatic services means they are often travelling. She has set them a challenge that they all enjoy.

Lady Royston invites them back in a fortnight's time, but Patsy and Norah will not be there, as they are attending the Patrol Leaders' and Seconds' Divisional Meeting. They are invited even though the company is suspended, and the three younger Marigolds, Biddie, Pixie and Mary, will be free to go to Lady Royston's.

The three go to Lady's Royston's to play with Andrea and have lunch and spend the morning helping restore the old sunken herb plot. It has been neglected for years and Lady Royston admits 'that but for Ellie and her Gipsy lore, it might well have gone on being neglected for a great many more.' Ellie has given them advice on the herbs, although Lady Royston dissuades them from trying out some of the gipsy remedies!

Andrea is bored after the morning working and after lunch persuades the three Guides to go to Chagleigh with her by bus to go to the pictures. The expedition is doomed, as first of all they miss the direct bus, and they have to change at Brenton, the next little town.

While waiting at Brenton they see a poor old man playing a fiddle for pennies and Andrea persuades him to let her play the violin, which she does skilfully and the man collects a 'harvest of pennies.'

They then catch the wrong bus, which takes them to Frensham Common, where there is a Fair. They spend all their money and have to walk the ten miles back to Stone House. There is a storm and the girls get very wet and mud-stained walking back. They receive help from a gipsy when they call for help, as Andrea speaks Romany, learnt from a gipsy nurse. They are lucky in finding a lift home and are met by anxious parents and Norah and Patsy, their Leader and Second.

Andrea has been ill and is taken ill again after the disastrous adventure and Lady Royston is very cross indeed with her and with the Guides.

Norah, already smarting under the fact that her patrol has made such fools of them selves, tries to apologise but it is no use and they are sent home with their parents.

When next at Mr Hewlett's tool shed for carpentry instruction Norah gives the Patrol a piece of her mind about their conduct, but tells them about the County Patrol Competition in three months. There will be problems with transport but they can only discuss this briefly as there is carpentry to be done. Mary excuses herself as her mother has a nursing job nearby and has two free hours for them to meet.

The rest of them are distracted when working and discuss their transport problem with Mr Hewlett. He has a contract to deliver gravel every month near to Barham Towers, where the Competition is to be held, and offers transport on his lorry. Jim will wait to bring them back.

Mary comes back and excitedly tells then that her mother is nursing Lady Royston's niece, Andrea, Lady Royston having remembered that Mary's mother is a nurse. Also Andrea has persuaded Lady Royston to forgive the Guides and they are invited to go back to Stone House on the Saturday.

When Norah visits Andrea a fortnight later Andrea says that she had led the younger Guides into trouble. She is older than them and should have thought ahead and been prepared as Norah would have done.

She says:

> "But now I want to be like you and learn to keep my head screwed on more. I think if I was a Guide it would help. It does, doesn't it?"
> "Yes," Norah is quite serious now. "It does, Andrea. You see – one doesn't bleat all the time about the Promise and the Laws, but they're always there, somehow, in the background, something to measure life up against, a standard to go by."

They agree to find out from Norah's Guide Captain how Andrea can be enrolled as a Lone Guide. Andrea tells Norah that when they were at the gipsy site, there was a caravan for sale and they agree to try to buy this for Ellie. To raise the money needed they will have a garden fete, at which Andrea, a gifted violinist, will play.

Lady Royston takes them over to see the caravan, which is still for sale at eighteen pounds. She also offers Mary and her mother the lodge at Stone House to rent, with Mrs Glover becoming the District Nurse. Mrs Glover has to work away for a while but afterwards will move to the lodge.

The fete is very successful and the head mistress of St Bridget's comes to see the sunken herb garden the Guides have worked on. She is very impressed and asks them about the Patrol Competition they are entering. She stays for Andrea's recital, which also gives great pleasure to Ellie, the gipsy. Norah finds Andrea in tears after the recital, as her father has been moved to another embassy. She has to leave the next day and is unhappy, as she so wants to be a Guide:

> For a long minute Norah sat very still, her arm round the other girl's shoulders, her face gone scared and grave. Then her grip tightened. With her free hand she unfastened the shining trefoil that held her pirate scarf in place.
>
> "Chief says in the Law, a Guide is a person who is honourable, loyal, obedient, kind. I reckon, Andy, you're a Guide now, whether anybody's ever enrolled you or not. I can't enrol you, because I'm not a Captain, but I'm giving you my badge, to prove that you count as one of us, with me."

The Marigold Patrol prepares very thoroughly for the Patrol Competition and checks all the equipment and uniform are in order. They leave on Mr Hewlett's lorry, with Jim Willox at the wheel. The load is of bright yellow gravel and Jim has covered it as best as he can to save the Guides' uniforms from being dirtied. On the way they have an accident in which their kit and uniforms are messed up and Jim has a broken leg. The chauffeur of the other vehicle involved goes to phone for an ambulance and the car owner comes to their help. After the ambulance has taken Jim to hospital they make their way to Barham Towers, by train, bus and a baker's cart with the little of their equipment they can salvage. They arrive late and not very smart, although they have done their best to tidy themselves and are allowed to enter the Competition.

They do their best and, although they receive no marks for inspection, they do well with the rest of the challenges. Lady Royston arrives, having heard of the accident from their builder friend, Mr Hewlett, and will stay to take them home after a campfire and the results.

Although they do not win the County Shield, they have been placed second and, as the County Commissioner announces this, she tells the audience about the road accident they have been in. She has heard about this from a witness to the accident, who has telephoned her. She also says they had been very efficient at the accident scene and presents them with a second prize, a framed copy of Margaret Tarrant's picture, ' The Adventurers.' This is applauded and they then go home with Lady Royston, who tells them that Andrea will be returning with her parents as her father has been given a London appointment. They will be living with her.

After the summer holidays Mr Hewlett and Jim help the Marigolds to fetch the caravan, which they have painted and fitted out, to the pitch Ellie the gipsy has chosen by a stream. They invent an errand to keep her busy while they do this and then go to have tea with Mary Glover. She is a different girl now she has a home with her mother and has had new glasses and a tidy hairdo. Norah says that Mary had helped at the motor accident by turning off the engine to prevent a fire as two of the Guides had been in the cab with Jim. This has been kept as a Patrol secret.

Andrea unfastens the trefoil badge belonging to Norah, worn behind her new school tie, and gives it back to her, asking that she can be enrolled with this badge:

> "Here, take it, I'd like to be enrolled with this one if I may," she said softly. " I've worn it all the time. Tomorrow I'll be able to wear it where it'll show."

They are going on to a company meeting called by their Captain, Miss Blagrove, at which Andrea and Mary will be enrolled. Miss Nesbitt, their headmistress, has written to the girls to let them know that the 6th Oakleigh Guides can continue:

> "Since, evidently, patrols can do good work on their own, without interfering with school activities or taking up an unfair share of the Guiders' time. I shall be delighted for St Bridget's Company to carry on. I consider that there is absolutely no question about it – the Guides have made good."

Fact or Fiction ?

I have been very lucky in making contact with a lady, Marion Pleydell, who, with her friend Betty, was one of Margaret Tennyson and Catherine Christian's Guides in Woldingham. Marion has most kindly written the following for me about Guiding there in the 1940's, when she felt the Woldingham Company had its most colourful existence. She said that beside their weekly Guide Meetings they were free to visit Margaret and Catherine in their gipsy caravan 'whenever the mood took us,' and they were always welcoming. This was in their spare time from their full time jobs in London. I am quoting this in full as I feel it has the full flavour of the best of Guiding at that time and as I am so impressed by the fullness of these ladies' recollections after sixty plus years.

> 'On the other side of the road there was an odd shaped plot, rough and uncultivated, next to The Hut with its orchard and cobnut trees. Just inside this field was a genuine brightly painted gypsy caravan, the home of Margaret Tennyson and Catherine Christian. They were respectively Captain and Lieutenant of the 1st Woldingham Guide Company, and in this wartime period there were enough young girls remaining in the village for two patrols, the Robins and the Wrens. In better weather meetings were held in yet another caravan, this time a more modern one, which was further down the field.
>
> Margaret Tennyson, the captain, was a great niece of Alfred Lord Tennyson. She was also Editor of 'The Guide', the publication for Guides worldwide. Catherine Christian's daytime job was as Editor

of the sister publication 'The Guider'. This meant that both women worked at Guide Headquarters in Buckingham Palace Road. All the Guiding offices in those days were in the upper floors over the Girl Guide shop, which is still in the same premises today. It also meant that we were frequent visitors to the London Headquarters. During wartime there was a fund-raising scheme for the G.I.S. It seems wrong now, but we would pick primroses, tie them into small bunches and then take them to Guide Headquarters in London to sell to those working in the offices, the money going into the G.I.S fund. Other frequent trips were to Purley (a town south of Croydon, now about a quarter of an hour's drive by car, but then needing two bus journeys so not straightforward by any means) where the Guides had an empty shop. Here we spent our time demolishing old spent batteries, a war effort activity, which was never explained to us, and I now think might have been quite hazardous!

Woldingham offered great adventure for youngsters in those days. As Guides we wandered for miles. We would go ' stalking and tracking,' memories too of one patrol climbing to the top of Nore Hill (about 800ft) and then semaphoring messages down to the other patrol waiting by the gypsy caravan. Best of all were the evenings when we held meetings in the Blue Chalet. Many houses in Woldingham are larger than the average. Several were requisitioned as billets for soldiers, mainly Canadians. Then there were empty houses either because their owners had fled to somewhere safer or else had left them because they had suffered war damage. We were close to two Battle of Britain airfields and also the village was on the flight path of enemy bombers and later V1s and V2s going towards London. While exploring we had discovered in a wood a large summer/garden house. Not sure what its original use had been but it was a two-storey wooden building, and always known to us as the Blue Chalet because it was painted a muted grey-blue, a colour that is known as Lutyens blue nowadays. Although appearing abandoned, the structure was sturdy and quite safe- even the upstairs. Guide meetings we held there always ended with a real camp fire and a good sing-song. To us, this was so romantic. It was totally different from other Guide companies meeting in church halls or similar premises. In fine weather our weekly meetings were held either in the caravan field or in the Blue Chalet.

One Guide camp we attended was at Foxlease (the Guide House in the New Forest), where there were many other Guide companies. Memories are of endless rain. As patrol leader I was responsible for such things as the guy ropes of the bell tent and before we left for home all my clothes were soaked, so that I ended up wearing some of Catherine's. Shows she must have been a small woman, as I've always been short and slim. However, despite the rain we did get to meet Lady Baden-Powell, then the Chief Guide.

Now I'll refer to friend Betty's notes. She says:

Thinking about it, I don't suppose our Company was ever more than fourteen or fifteen in number at the most; perhaps not even that. An elite band!

Yes. The Blue Chalet was special. On one Sunday we were used as war invasion casualties and the Blue Chalet was part of that exercise. It must have been in conjunction with the A.R.P., the Home Guard, Red Cross etc. Some of the injuries were made gory using meat bones sticking through lisle stockings. Once we were found we were given first aid, but what happened then I am not sure.

I can remember more about preparations to go to camp than I can about Foxlease itself. I do remember having new blue winceyette pyjamas to go, which must have been a struggle with clothing coupons – and the army blankets, which we learnt how to fold as sleeping bags.

Thinking back, although it was wartime we led remarkably normal lives. Trips to London must have left our parents feeling apprehensive, but at that stage air raids were probably mainly at night. One visit to Guide Headquarters coincided with a visit from Princess Elizabeth as she was then. I know I managed to clamber up on something to get a better view of her in her Ranger's uniform.

On another occasion we went to the theatre and I do know it was my first trip to a London theatre (I too remember this. The show was called something, which had 'Rainbow' in the title, and we spent the night on the floor in a flat just round the corner from Guide Headquarters. M.)

There must have been a time in the winter when it was quite difficult to find somewhere to meet that could have heating, because the parents of one Guide let us use their day nursery, a huge room with a dumb waiter. And occasionally we were allowed to use the church hall.

I suppose being wartime, our activities were also geared towards coping with just that, " Be Prepared". I know we were well practised in the art of dressing in complete blackout. Not an easy exercise with all the bits and pieces making up our uniforms. But there was keen competition between the patrols to improve on our time.

With regards to the religious side of Guiding, as far as I remember Thinking Day was when we were allowed to wear our Guide uniforms to school, but I don't remember any more than this. I do, however, remember church parades for Armistice Day when some of us marched to church for the remembrance service along with the British Legion, Home Guard etc. (My parents were anti this side of Guides, so I wasn't allowed to attend any church activities. M.) I was never the flag bearer.

I hope this account has some value. As we keep stressing, we did feel 'different' in our Guiding years. Other companies didn't seem to have such colourful Captains or Lieutenants, nor meet in such romantic settings. I was a huge Arthur Ransome fan, and to me all our Guiding activities dovetailed with the concept his books contained about being out of doors and having fun and adventures. Very happy times, despite the War.'

Marion Pleydell, *September 2008, with a huge input from friend Betty.*

Guide International Service (G.I.S)

As this is mentioned early in Marion's account I think I should explain as it may be a new term to many people and as this is a good example of valuable work undertaken by Guides in Wartime, loyal to the Guide Movement and being useful and helping others in this period.

During the Second World War, as early as 1939, as refugees started to arrive in the UK, Guides began to write to Headquarters asking if something could be done for people in the invaded countries of Europe. It was impossible while the War was still taking place, but plans began to be made for an 'Army of Good Will.'

A list was made of voluntary organisations prepared to give help in relief work in Europe at the end of the War and the Guide Association was the third group to apply after the Red Cross and Society of Friends.

It was known that conditions in Europe would be bad and help would be needed.

Guides set about earning the money for a Fund to finance the Guides' part and many women applied to be part of a team to go when possible. By 1945 over £150,000 had been raised and training had been given to those selected. The first team left in 1944 for Greece and the second, a hospital team, went to Holland on the day it was liberated.

By VE Day, 8th May 1945, the end of the War in Europe, there were G.I.S Teams working in two of the worse devastated countries, and others ready for service.

In the story 'The Marigolds Make Good' a Guide Patrol has decided to continue as Guides after their school has closed the Guide Company for a time. They set out to prove that they can achieve good Guiding on their own and so show their loyalty to their Patrol, Guide Company and School.

A Guide in the 1920's and 1930's would have accepted this law, her loyalty being to King and Country as well as to friends, family, School and to her Guide Company.

I am sure that Patrols continued to meet on their own or in their homes, particularly when, as in war-time, halls where they had met were not available – the local church hall where I live was intended to be used in the Second World War as a rest centre for evacuees from Birmingham. It was set out with bedding, urns and so on, but was fortunately never needed. Similarly someone then a Scout told me that in the dark days of 1940, when people felt invasion was imminent, his Scout Leader announced that they were no longer to meet in the foreseeable future. This was largely due to Invasion fears and the belief that boys in an organisation like Scouts would be drafted into the Hitler Youth Movement. He had arranged for them to have some Civil Defence lectures and said good-bye to them asking that they keep their Scout Promise.

Guides worked for the War Effort with fund-raising and salvage collections. The Guide Association raised enough money to fund motor ambulances and even a lifeboat, 'The Guide of Dunkirk', used in its unfinished state at Dunkirk.

In the Channel Islands and Malta Guides also were acknowledged for their War Effort, in the Channel Islands Guides went 'underground', meeting in secret and hiding their precious flags until they were free.

In the 1930's, at the time 'The Marigolds Make Good', was written, in the small Worcestershire villages of Martley and Knightwick and around, patrols of Sea Rangers were set up a long way away from the sea. Their loyalty to their country and patrols was shown in their logbook and letters that I have thanks to Miss Mary Walker, who was one of these girls. Mary was a lifelong Guide, involved in the Movement as a girl and adult – and kindly gave me uniforms dating to the 1920's for our Guide Archives, including two original Guide hats from the 1920's and 1930's. She kept her own hat to wear for gardening!

Their logbook for 1931 records a meeting on December 7th at 8.30 p.m. in the Memorial Hall. Girls (most of whom were already Guides) met from several villages.

Minutes
Miss Dickinson was asked to take the chair.
Miss Richerton acted as secretary.
Mrs C. Winnington was the speaker.
Miss Dickinson asked the meeting to consider whether we should have Rangers or Sea Rangers.

1. It was unanimously voted that we should start Rangers.

2. The next question was to decide whether we were to be Sea Rangers or Rangers – Ranger Promise of service in the wider world. It was decided to be Sea Rangers unanimously. It was suggested that we call ourselves 1. Temeraire , or 2. Golden Hind. More suggestions for names next week.

3. It was suggested we meet once a week in each village, but once a month altogether at Martley – Red Cross at the big meeting and then at each village a special form of work most favoured by each Patrol.

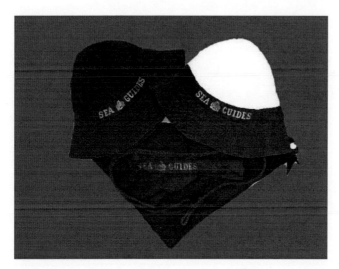

Part of the uniform – winter and summer hats, with tally bands and early title as Sea Guides, neckerchief and lanyard.

The first meeting at Martley took place on 15th December 1931 7-9 p.m. – under the name of S.R.S. Worcester, with Captain, Mrs C Winnington, 1st Lieutenant Mrs J Walker and 2nd Lieutenant Miss Dickinson (also Paymaster). 7 other girls made up the patrol with appropriate Naval titles (sick bay, ship's writer etc).

Important letters were copied in their logbook and a letter had been sent to the Thames Nautical Training College, H.M.S.Worcester,(off Greenhithe)asking permission to use their title for the Sea Ranger 'ship'. The return letter dated 14/1/1932 to Mrs C Winnington read:-

It is with much pleasure I learn that the Worcestershire Girl Guides wish to call their Sea Ranger Ship the Worcester, after our training ship, and we readily give our consent.

I should like to make a small presentation to mark the occasion, and should like your advice as to the most suitable form – either an ensign, framed pictures, book (the History of the Worcester) or a couple of dozen Worcester booklets.
Please let me know, wishing the Guides all success.

Yours truly
G Stub Commander R.N. Captain Superintendent.

The reply on 15/1, 1932 read:

Dear Sir,
Thank you very much for your kind letter, and for your consent to our calling SRS Worcester after the great training ship. We are most grateful and very much encouraged. We shall feel very honoured indeed to accept your offer of an ensign and I thank you for the presentation with the greatest sincerity.
If it is possible to purchase a picture of the Worcester and the book (the History of the Worcester) I will gladly buy them for the SR ship - again thanking you for your kindness and help.

Yours truly
Charlotte Winnington

Despite problems over a meeting place this Ranger Patrol, and the Company Meeting monthly, modelled them-selves on a ship.

At their third muster at Hill House, Shelsley Beauchamp, with 24 girls and officers present:

Dr. Green gave a 2nd lecture and we did a great deal of bandaging. Miss Olive Lewis taught first lesson on Hornpipe. First routine of ship was fixed:

Each Sea Ranger coming 'aboard' salutes, stands a moment, smiles and goes to form her 'watch.'

When visitors arrive one watch in turn beginning with the starport will receive the visitor and see him or her off.

Subsequent correspondence from the Commander dated 6/2/1932 gives an insight into the age range of the college and what was expected of the young sailors.

The letter to Mrs Charles Winnington M.B.E reads:

Dear Madam,

I have made all the arrangements for the Presentation of our Flag on Saturday, 27ᵗʰ February, and hope these are suitable to you.

Cadet Keith Malcolm Davis, age 14 and a half, will represent the 'Worcester'.

He will leave Paddington 9.45 a.m. Saturday 27ᵗʰ, arriving at Worcester 12.43 p.m.. If you will kindly put him up for the night, he could catch the 10.25 a.m. train from Worcester Sunday, arriving Paddington 2.40 p.m.

I wish to confirm that the Flag will not be on a staff, but will be ceremonially hoisted on a mast or staff.

Cadet Davis will hand the Flag, picture and Book with our greetings and good wishes. He will salute the flag as it is hoisted by one of your Guides.

Cadet Davis will be well able to look after himself in every way, and will have his uniform evening dress with him as well as his day uniform

Yours faithfully
Commander.

The Head of Sea Rangers, the Ranger Pilot Miss d'Avigdor, wrote to Mrs Winnington on 12/2/1932 from Guide Imperial Headquarters in Buckingham Palace Road to check the arrangements for the Flag Presentation, to which she had been invited.

She wanted to know if she was to make a speech as "I am not very good at impromptu speaking."

She suggested she should get together with the Rangers afterwards and perhaps have some Sea Ranger Games.

The event took place with due ceremony and is recorded in the logbook:

February 27ᵗʰ 1932. Presentation at Brockhill Court.

Cadet Keith Malcolm Davis – on behalf of Commander Steele

R/U V.R.- presented the ensign, engraving of the H.M.S. Worcester and history, to the Division Commissioner, Miss A Judson. The ensign was hoisted and saluted – God Save the King sung – 3 Cheers were given for H.M.S. Worcester.

Miss d'Avigdor, the Ranger Pilot, came and enrolled eleven members of the Crew. Admiral Cumings made a splendid speech and said we were now attached to the Mercantile Marine and it was a great honour.

Other local Guide officers were there and the Ranger Pilot taught 'delightful games'. The ensign was lowered at the end of the meeting.

The Ensign of H.M.S Worcester presented to the Sea Rangers

By July 1932 Mrs Winnington was writing to 'the Crew' as follows:

On January 27th our Ship started on her voyage with a splendid send off. Previous to that we had started our First Aid classes. Then we came into our first real bad storm – the loss of our nice quarters at the Memorial Hall, Martley, and the loss of our Paymaster, Miss Dickinson.
Since then we have had many difficulties, and some have, at least for the present, been unable to come aboard.

Now, S.R.S.Worcester was founded to be the centre of training for good and faithful citizenship and to make the lives of the girls of Martley and District full of joyous, faithful service to GOD and King and Country, and to learn to be skilful in such things as First Aid and Navy Craft besides being good shipmates.

Both your Lieutenant and I find ourselves very busy with home duties and pressing obligations, but we are most anxious that the ship should carry on. I am asking that the Patrol Leaders will come and meet here, at

Hill House, on Wednesday, July 10th, 5.30 to 9 o'clock, business meeting 7 o'clock, and all the members of the crew who can come. Or, will you settle in each Boat's Crew at your own village, what is best to do and the Leader report your decision.

Remember that Zeal and alacrity are two marks of a good Sea Ranger, and of the grand merchant seamen under whose flag we have the great privilege to serve.

With very best wishes
Your Captain, Charlotte Winnington.

P.S. I have hopes of nice quarters in the Autumn.

It is recorded that Mrs Winnington had to retire as Sea Ranger Captain and also District Commissioner through ill health. Mrs John Walker took over as Acting Captain.

The Sea Ranger Unit was still successful in 1938, when the Sea Rangers joined others on 'Implacable', a Training Ship. 300 girls were trained in Seamanship and this included training for Sea Guiders. Bearing in mind the nearness of the Second World War, it is to be wondered how many of these girls were able to put their knowledge to good use. It is known that during the War Years girls were anxious to be Sea Rangers as this would give them an advantage in applying to join the Wrens.

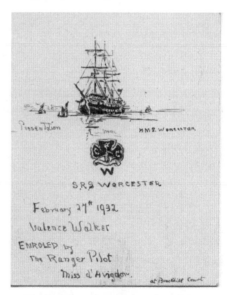

Among the memorabilia still in good order for this Ranger Ship are the History of the Worcester, a Manual of Seamanship, a booklet on the Training College, its Annual Report and list of prizes for 1934 and pictures of the College, also the Flag given to them.

Sea Rangers Enrolment Certificate.
Miss (Valence) Mary Walker

Chapter 6

The Third Guide Law
'A Guide's Duty is to be Useful and to help others'

Judy, Patrol Leader - by Dorothea Moore

A book most book-collectors and older Guide people will have read or heard of is this book by Dorothea Moore, which is the reason I am including the story. I only have this in the Children's Press edition dating from the 1950's, which I received as a Guide then. The original book was printed by Collins in 1930, although my copy has a dust-wrapper showing uniform from the 1950's with the Guide blue blouses, rather than the navy dress or blouse of the 1930's.

Re-reading this book, which is not considered by some to be a well-written story, I am sure that at eleven or twelve even I would have thought it a good read and full of derring-do!

The dustwrapper of my 1950's edition.

The Judy of the title, Judy Bethune, is fourteen years old, small for her age and pretty, and already a Guide when the story begins.

The book tells the story of how she becomes a daygirl at the boarding school, St.Oswyth's, the feats of heroism she performs using her Guide knowledge, and how when the school forms a Guide Company she is a Patrol Leader. She is naturally a leading light in the Company.

At the beginning of the book Mr James Bethune D.S.O. is working as the Classics Master at St. Oswyths, the chief girls' school in Merchester. By day he teaches Latin to girls who loathe the subject and give him no replies in class; outside school hours he lives, quite literally, the other side of the school wall. He lodges with a Mrs Petticum at Carlton House, where food is badly cooked and meagre. Having been left with a limp after the War, he has found it hard to find employment, needing to support himself and an orphaned niece in the Orkneys.

His staid life (and that of his un-obliging landlady) is changed abruptly by the arrival out of the blue of his niece Jacobina, "Judy to my friends though."

She has lost her lodgings in the Orkneys, when Mrs McKay, her hostess there, needs to travel to the Malay States to care for her son's baby after his wife's death. Judy handles the landlady far better than her uncle does, offering help, doing some cookery, making herself useful and keeping her Guide Law:

"Perhaps you think I can't cook," Judy said. "But I can, quite well. You'll just see. Are you having cold mutton like Uncle Jimmy? You'll see what a stew I'll turn you out – and may I do ours at the same time? It won't cost any more fire."

"It's the gal's night out – there's no one to show you anything," Mrs Petticum flung at her, in a "That-will-settle-you-miss" tone of voice.

"You bet I'll find everything I want – I'm a Guide," Judy assured her brightly and disappeared with promptitude. Mrs Petticum gazed blankly for a second at the door, and then decided to finish the room before going in pursuit and mentioning "sharpish" what she thought of her new lodger's "imperence."

It took her nearly twenty minutes to finish the room however, and by the time she arrived downstairs an extraordinary savoury smell was coming from the kitchen to greet her. Obviously, Mrs Petticum realised with amazement, this astonishing child was as good as her word, and had a notion of cooking.

Judy is up with the lark on her first morning there – well at 6.45 anyway and goes out to explore. She decides to take a look at her new school, St

Oswyth's, climbing in over the wall. She finds a way to enter the buildings and while doing this spots a burglar. Waking a pupil up she suggests that she tells the headmistress, Miss Salway, while she watches the burglar packing school silver away. She locks him in the pantry and tells the headmistress, enjoying a cup of tea with her while waiting for the police. She talks to the police and is back in bed for an hour's sleep before breakfast!

The story is duly told to her startled uncle, Mr Bethune, who only now realises how his life has changed with the arrival of Judy, his niece. The two of them now pay a formal visit to the headmistress and Judy is accepted in form IVA. She is taken to meet the other girls at Assembly:

> Miss Salway walked out. Form after form filed out after her in a most orderly manner. Judy was left with Form IVA – in it but not of it. She stood near the group of girls, wondering when one of them would speak of her.
>
> One spoke, but not to her, " Jolly good cheek of old Dry-dust to plant his belongings on us."
>
> Judy suddenly realised that the speech referred to Uncle Jimmy and her-self.

In the Latin lesson she goes on to further upset the class by answering her uncle's questions, as the uninterested class choose not to answer any. She now understands why her uncle looks so tired and harassed. The only kindness shown to her is by Maura Briarly, the girl she had woken the previous day when she climbed into the school. She is invited to go down to the sea with Maura and a friend on their half-day but has to refuse as she is going out with her uncle.

Judy and her uncle travel by bus to Greenfell Head and then walk for a time, but Uncle Jimmy is happy to sit and read while Judy explores. She returns to find him asleep and decides to walk in the other direction where there are cliffs above a small cove. Her uncle has warned her that the tide comes in very quickly and, as the sea is now further in than when they came, she doesn't go down to the beach. However she sees a hanky being waved and, looking down, sees two schoolgirls crouching in the lee of the cliffs:

It did not take Judy more than half a minute to make up her mind what must be done and done at once. Above high-water mark the cliff might be climbable; she thought it was – for herself at least – but not the most hopeful person in any world could see a way of getting up that first smooth fifteen or twenty feet. The coastguard cottages and the ropes always kept there were the one hope.

She runs to tell her uncle and runs off to the coastguard cottages, which she had called at earlier, and hopes to find a man to help and a strong rope. The coastguard's wife tells her that her husband and his mate are away overhauling a shed of stores. She sends her son to fetch them and goes with Judy to help,

"I doubt if I'd be strong enough to pull the young ladies up by myself," the coastguard's wife said; " but I would try if they knew how to fasten a rope that'll hold, round themselves. But not one in a thousand can do that; it needs a man to go down to them. Unless the rope holds it is sheer murder to try and pull them up over the cliff face, my dear."

"Oh, that's all right then," Judy said joyfully. "My Uncle Jimmy is there to help you pull them up, and I'll go down and tie the ropes for them. I know about knots; I'm a Guide."

Judy manages to climb down the cliff with the rope tied round her and reaches the two girls, Maura and Nancy, who are by now knee deep in water. She ties the rope round Nancy and she is pulled to safety and by the time the rope is lowered down to them the water is waist deep. She ties the rope round Maura and tries to hold on her-self to be rescued:

The sun had gone behind a cloud, and the wind was higher, sweeping in waves that had seemed unpleasantly big, when you were clinging to a slippery cliff that had nothing on it to cling to, and trying to keep an unsteady foothold on sand that was being sucked from under your feet

It wasn't pleasant, but it was something to have been Guide enough to know the knots that saved the lives of two girls. Judy braced herself up, to hold and endure; saying over and over to herself lines that her father had taught her long ago;

" If you can force your heart and nerve and sinew
To serve your turn long after they are gone,
And still hold on, when there is nothing in you
Except the will that says to you, hold on!"

The rope is lowered back down sooner that she has hoped, as Maura has untied herself and hangs on part way up, waiting for Judy:

"You were sport to do that!" she exclaimed, as she knelt down beside Maura, with a ·steadying hand on her elbow. "It was getting a bit uncomfortable down there, when the rope came."

"Did you think I was going to leave you to drown, because we didn't know how to tie a Guide knot at St. Oswyth's?" Maura asked rather shakily, and then she let Judy secure the rope around her again in silence.

" Help, help ! "

Judy and the cliff rescue.

Judy climbs the rest of the way to warm herself up and, only when she is safely up, do they see a boat being rowed into the cove by the coastguards. But for all their efforts, it would have come too late.

Judy and her uncle return home to Mrs Petticum, who has provided a clean tablecloth and cooked sausages for them.

Six St. Oswyth's girls come as a deputation to apologise for being beasts to both of them:

"We've passed a resolution to like Latin if we can, and we six are going to Miss Salway to ask if we may start a Guide Company at St. Oswyth's right away – and learn to tie knots and a few other things as well."

74

A notice about starting a Guide Company is put up at school by the head-girl, Clare, but this is not well received by Erica Finlayson, who is envious of Judy having an influence on Clare. Clare has previously been kind and encouraging to Erica. Erica persuades the others to vote against starting Guides.

Judy decides to walk off her disappointment, passing two former coastguards' cottages tucked under a crumbling cliff. A man rushes from one of the cottages and is going for the doctor for his baby who is having a fit, so Judy runs to the cottage to help:

> Judy fairly raced up that last bit of shingle to the shabby, blistered door, the paintless door belonging to the cottage which had smoke issuing from its chimney. That, of course, must be the cottage from which the poor man had come. And as she ran she went over anxiously in her mind the Guide First Aid that she had learned with the Ambulance Class, though her Captain had considered her too young as yet to try for the badges.

Entering she sees the baby, lying stiffly in a washing basket, serving as a cradle, with a small, lame, little boy trying to help. Judy manages with the boy's help, to find a washing tub and to pour in some hot water, making a warm bath for the baby, who recovers. It is hard to pull the tub out of the cupboard where it is in a pile of household utensils which falls down, but Judy concentrates on the baby. However when she is looking for a towel to dry the baby the cliff falls in on the cottage.

The girls at St. Oswyth's hear the sound of the rock fall and Judy's Uncle Jimmy comes to find her, but is told she left earlier. The headmistress, Miss Salway, returns from a meeting at the Town Hall and has heard of a 'frightful fall of cliff in Purdock's Bay.' A ragged man (the one Judy had met earlier) comes to the school for help for his baby, as the doctor is not available.

Miss Salway offers help:

> "Don't trouble any more; I'll find a doctor, and come down with him myself to bring some things for baby," she said kindly. " Of course you must hurry back to her at once; you left her alone, you say, with

only your little lame boy?"

"No'm; she ain't alone with him; seeing as a young lady she went along to see what she could do for my little 'un – a young lady as is one of them Girl Guides, what was uncommon handy round where I used to live, before I lost my job and come here."

"A Girl Guide"; Erica was not to get away from that term, it seemed.

Mr Bethune is relieved to hear that Judy is there, but alarmed when he discovers that the cottage is one of those under the cliff – which has just fallen.

The rescue party led by Mr Bethune goes to the cottages to dig Judy, the small boy and the baby out. Judy meantime has come round after the rock fall and managed to find the two children and to keep them safe, finding some water and milk for the baby and some bread to make a small amount of bread and milk. She has realised that they are buried, but has found a candle and sees that it is burning down on one side, so there is a draught and they are not completely shut in. Patient Judy sits down on a pile of fallen stones, and whistles the famous Guide song "Found a peanut."

Mr Bethune is relieved to hear her whistling and the men dig Judy and the children out:

Judy's voice came out some time before Judy herself could do so. However, and what she said was; " Please tell Billy's father that the baby came out of her fit. One up for the *Child Nurse Badge*!"

Following this adventure Clare, the Head girl at St. Oswyth's, calls another meeting at the school about starting Guides. Erica admits that she has told lies to persuade them against starting Guides and that she thinks they should now take the chance to begin. She intends to put her name down and to apologise to Judy and to ask her to teach her some knots.

A month later the Guide Company is up and running with Miss Relton as Captain and has seven Patrols, three of the Leaders being Judy, Clare and Maura. The Divisional Commissioner enrols the Guides with the usual ceremony and then:

It was over, the last Guide had saluted her Queen's Colours, and had been turned by the Commissioner to face the rest. Miss Relton changed the wording of her " Guides, salute," to the proud " Company, salute!" which could now be said at St.Oswyth's.

The Commissioner stood smiling down at the newly formed Company, when the Queen's Colours had been marched off, with forty-nine Guides standing at the salute.

Then she spoke.

When she had finished, there was a tiny pause, and then she raised her voice like a trumpet-call. "Patrol Leader Judy Bethune, forward march!"

Judy scrambled to her feet and marched up, looking startled. The Commissioner held out her hand.

"I have to pass on a handshake of congratulation from the Chief Guide," she said. "Your name has gone up to headquarters for fine service, but what matters is that when the call for service came you did not fail. Guides of St Oswyth's, I want three of your best cheers for Patrol-Leader Judy Bethune."

They gave them with a will – and a three times three.

The new Guide Company is hoping to camp for the last weekend of term but cannot find a suitable site. The ordinary campsite is fully booked and they have tried to arrange to camp at Senning Park, but the owner, Sir George Senning, has refused permission. His reason is given as that he 'won't have noisy schoolgirls playing at soldiers in his park.'

Judy's uncle, Mr Bethune, is going to visit Kingsbury, who was his batman in the War and lives near Senning. Judy goes with him and will have some time to spend on her own. Unsurprisingly she decides, without telling her uncle, to visit Sir George Senning to see if she can persuade him to change his mind. The lodge-keeper reluctantly lets her through into the grounds of Senning Park and she hurries to the house, meeting an old man she takes to be the gardener. He suggests she rings the bell and asks the butler, but says that Sir George doesn't trouble himself to see children.

The butler finally lets her in and asks her to wait in the hall, then takes her to see Sir George, who is the old man she had assumed was the gardener.

She has no luck in persuading him to let the Guides camp, although he says that if he sees with his own eyes that Guides are some good he may re-consider.

She decides to take a short cut through the grounds and over a wall and stops to look at a pond. She hears angry shouting and sees Sir George waving his stick at her and he threatens to set his dogs on her if she trespasses in the park again.

Judy climbs onto the wall to leave and, looking down the road to the village, sees her uncle coming out of a cottage. She shouts "Coo-ee!" to him and thinks she hears a faint echo behind her. Her uncle looks mystified as he cannot see where the shout originates, but before Judy can shout again she hears the cry again, which she thought was an echo. She goes back into the grounds and finds that Sir George has slipped into the pond and she manages to save him by keeping his head above water until her uncle Jimmy arrives to help.

Sir George withdraws his objections to the Guide camp and they have a good camp.

On a wet day her uncle shows her family papers about her namesake, Jacobina, who on her marriage was given family jewels, which were stolen by highwaymen. If ever found these would belong to Uncle Jimmy (and ease his poverty!).

She has one further adventure when she goes to stay for three weeks with her friend Maura, which involves them being put on a train in London to travel to Dunsterby. A strange old lady travels with them and, when there is a de-railment, Maura recognises the area and they leave the train to make their own way, accompanied by the old lady. They leave her to rest by a windmill and find a Post Office to send a telegram home and buy some buns and sweets.

On the way back to the windmill and old lady Judy finds her ancestress, Jacobina's grave. They explore the windmill, looking for the old lady who has vanished. Judy finds a secret passage and the clothes the old lady had worn, evidently a disguise. Hearing voices they hide in a hole in the wall and overhear enough to tell them that the old lady was a criminal in disguise.

As they try to leave the hole after the men have gone Judy dislodges a large stone and some earth and they fall into a pit. Judy searches for her lost torch and finds in some rotten red material some jewellery she thinks may have been Jacobina's stolen jewellery. This was in the right area, Ritchling Commmon.

They find an old document with a witch's curse that would bring ill luck on anyone finding the jewellery except the rightful owner.

They are stopped from climbing out of the pit when the criminal/old lady finds them there. He does not want to harm them and will help them out of the passage if they promise to say nothing until the next day. The girls will not agree and he jumps down and ties their hands behind their backs but Judy manages to conceal the jewellery. After he has left they manage to free themselves and climb out, aiming to go to Lullington Police Station. Maura's father has come to look for them and they hear his car horn and find he has brought the Police.

Craddock of the Yard had been hunting the gang of criminals and he is grateful to the girls as the men have now been arrested.

The jewellery now belonging to Uncle Jimmy is sold and the £90,000 raised means that Uncle Jimmy can thankfully resign as Latin master. They can also find a home of their own and Judy can become a boarder at St. Oswyth's, sharing a room with Maura.

Fact or Fiction ?

There is no doubt that Judy Bethune leads a very exciting life and that opportunities present themselves for her to be a heroine. However there is no doubt either that she believes totally in the third Guide Law and her natural wish to be helpful always comes to the fore.

I doubt that any one Guide of the 1930's or even the 1950's, when I first read this book, could have had all these adventures. I would have loved to have the chance to do all these things, but for most girls they would be only in their imagination.

Judy's Uncle Jimmy may well have been, as many men were, forced into uncongenial jobs by their circumstances. Girls who were day girls at Boarding Schools under Judy's circumstances may well have been scorned by their fellow pupils and not every school would have gone wholeheartedly into Guiding, although the Boarding Schools were the cradle of Guiding in many places. Their headmistresses, being ideal for Commissioners, were among the first to open Guide companies in their schools.

In my small village the village company was 5th Malvern Wells, the companies numbered 1 to 4 and in fact the 6th were all at the Abbey School.

Judy Bethune is probably the Guide we would have liked to be, but Guides of the time had plenty of opportunities for doing their duty and helping others, whether it was by raising money for orphans or knitting garments for poor children.

In the Guide Movement there has also always been the readiness to put the good of others before yourself – and as the Brownies would be told at their enrolment, "I trust you to keep your Promise and to do at least one good turn every day."

The 'Good Turn' has always been part of Guiding and challenges often required you to list your Good Turns for the week. Even as adults we never think what it is that propels us forward to be the one to help if a child is lost in a shop, an old lady needs a hand onto the bus (no- not across the road unless she wants to go!) or to be the one who takes charge in an emergency. After all we have always had in our Brownie or Guide pocket the money to make a public phone call – along with a clean hanky, a safety pin, a plaster and pencil and paper. We are conditioned to carry these, except that now we have fewer pockets and a mobile phone would be the essential item for many of us!

Chapter 7

The Fourth Guide Law
'A Guide is a Friend to All and a Sister to every Other Guide'

Judy Joins the Jasmines - by Elizabeth Mumford

This Guide Law is well illustrated in the slender volume of Elizabeth Mumford's 'Judy Joins the Jasmines', published in 1934 by C.S.S.M. My slightly worn copy was printed with binding to the authorised Economy Standard (War-time) and presented to Dorothy Thompson by Charles Street Sunday school, Worcester, on 31ˢᵗ December 1943.

I have been unable to find out anything about the author, other than that the name appears to be a pseudonym and that her books fall roughly within the term of Evangelical School Stories. These are books aiming to convert the unconverted and encourage those committed to a faith. This book was given as a Sunday School prize although its well-read state must mean that it was well loved by someone, and read rather more than the few times you might anticipate.

The story is that of Judy Stanisford who lives with her sick mother in Cradborough, her mother having gone 'all to bits' after her husband's death. Judy has attended the Russell day school and enjoyed its sports and being a member of its Guide Company. She now finds that she is to leave all this to go to a boarding school, Hadley Court, where an old friend of her mother's, Miss Fairlie, is Principal. Her mother is to go to a Hydro in Germany for treatment. While Judy is sorry to leave her school and friends, she goes willingly in the hope that her mother's health will improve.

In a chance meeting in a local park, when a dog runs up to her, she has a brief conversation with two girls and, when she is on the train to school, she meets one of them, Sheila Massinger, again. Sheila talks to other friends and Judy tries not to hear their conversation, but Sheila then recognises her as the 'Girl-in-the-Park'. The others introduce themselves, discover that Judy is a Guide as they are and at once make friends. They have a school Guide Company she can join.

Sheila has a Russian friend at school called Anna, who becomes jealous of Judy as her friendship with Sheila grows. All three girls are put into a small dormitory together, while Anna wants only to share with Sheila.

The new Guide Lieutenant is Frances Gardiner, the other girl from the park at home, a former head girl who has come back to teach while a teacher is away.

The story is largely about the ups and downs of the three's friendship, but contains quite a lot about Guide drill and meetings.

Problems arise again when Anna is put into the Clover Patrol while Judy joins the Jasmines, where Sheila is Patrol Leader.

At Guide camp, after a confrontation with Anna, Judy and Sheila go to the beach and Sheila confides in sympathetic Frances Gardiner, who joins them, about how her friendship with Judy has upset Anna:

"Fran, I want your Guiderly advice," she began.

Frances smiled. " You shall have it- I'll be all auntly! … What's the problem?"

"Oh!" Judy exclaimed startled. " Shall I go?"

"No, Judy- stay. You'll help … but, Fran, you must promise to be serious- and not to laugh at me. Don't even laugh inside!"

"I won't," said Frances gently. " I never laugh about – worries; you know that. Tell me; I'd love to help if I can."

Sheila sat with bent head, sifting the sand between her fingers. "It's Anna."

"Yes?" said Frances and waited.

"When she first came to school, over a year ago now, she was shy and lonely and not a bit happy, and I – I tried to be friends with her. She's awfully nice in many ways… Then I found out she was going too far. She was getting almost too much friends." Sheila was crimson, but she went on bravely. " She wanted me all the time; she wasn't happy unless she was with me. It was – difficult."

Frances nodded, but said nothing.

"Well, then Judy came to school, and from the first we seemed fated to be friends- didn't we, Ju? She was put in Little Dorm with Anna and me. She was placed next to me in class. We were constantly being- almost shoved at one another. And it hurt Anna, of course. Things got worse and worse, till today we had a regular row, all three of us. It didn't seem right, to give in to Anna; I couldn't give in to her about being friends with other people, could I, Frances? 'Twouldn't have been good for her. If she'd been willing to have a trio – herself, Judy, and me –"

Frances looked at Judy. " Would *you* have wanted a 'trio '– honestly, Judy ? "

Frances gives advice to
Judy and Sheila

Judy is asked to look at it from Anna's point of view, which she does, and agrees she wouldn't have wanted a 'trio' had she been in Anna's place.

Frances talks this over with them, and then suggests that Sheila at 16 is now Ranger age and the keynote of Rangers is Service.

"Rangers is to help girls to help other people."

She feels Sheila has tried to help Anna, but Sheila feels that she has muddled it up:

Frances says " We all muddle up things sometimes, especially if we're trying to do things off our own bat – if we haven't got God's guidance."

They discuss this and Frances tells them that you can only discover the secret of true service through asking Jesus into your life. Sheila says she will do this and Judy knows that she has reached a milestone in her life and:

'In the silence, in her silent heart, Judy yielded her life to her Master'.

On the next day Judy and three others (not Sheila as being the Patrol Leader she is experienced), go on a hike, travelling one way by train. Judy asks Anna to join them, which she has refused, but they meet her in a shop and she now agrees to come, although reluctantly. The hike back planned by Judy goes well at first; they light a fire and cook sausages and, despite the clouded skies, enjoy laying and following a trail. When it starts to rain they find shelter in the woods until the thunder comes just as they are trying to reach the outskirts of the wood.

However lightning strikes a tree and the falling branches catch Judy. Anna deals with moving her to a shed and bandages a gash on Judy's forehead. She then runs for help, having to go through a railway tunnel, only avoiding being hit by a train by sliding into a manhole in the tunnel.

Judy recovers from her injuries at a farmhouse and is allowed to go to camp on the last day, staying in the Hospital tent. The Guides preparing for the ' Make- Your –Own-Clothes' Party pop in and out to see her and Anna comes on her own. Judy thanks her:

There was a terrible crashing, rending sound, and a tree fell across her path.

(See page 138.)

Judy and friends shelter in a thunderstorm

"You've been splendid, Anna. I heard all about the way you went so nobly to fetch help, though you were absolutely done in your self."

"It wasn't noble at all…. Oh, Judy, I wish we had not been such foes before. It was just because I was – silly- and jealous."

Judy crimsoned. "Rot, Anna. It was my fault, too...... I wanted Sheila for my friend, all to myself – yes, I did, underneath, though I wouldn't own it for ages, even to myself... I was horribly selfish... My only excuse is that I was- lonely at first- and Sheila helped me so much..."

Anna tells Judy how Sheila has helped her too, after her mother's illness and death, when she has been so unhappy at school. Judy tells Anna about her own worries for her mother's health:

Anna gasped suddenly. " Judy! Oh, Judy- and I've been so horrid. Judy, I   never dreamed -! Oh! - I'm so sorry!"
And in that moment there was a very thorough reconciliation between them.

Judy tells Anna that her mother is now recovering and that she is thankful to God. She helps Anna too to ask Jesus Christ to come into her heart.

"It would be – topping, Anna, if He were Best Friend to all three of us, and we were His friends as well as one another's".
And so it happened that the friendship of three girls was cemented in the unity of their friendship with the truest friend of all.

Fact or Fiction ?

This book is not only about girls' friendships, but introduces, in an unsentimental way, the friendship girls can have with Jesus Christ.

Indeed the Guide Promise has always included the commitment to 'do my duty to God' or in today's wording 'to love my God.' For Guides in the late 1930's and early 1940's the introduction of a religious element in a book would have been quite normal. You only need to read the books given as Sunday school prizes then, and incidentally right into the 1950's and early 1960's.

Most girls then would have been very comfortable with this, having the topic well covered in school and at Sunday school. They would almost certainly attend a church and would expect to be confirmed and married there, to have their children christened and to bring them up the same way.

Guide companies early on were often linked with a church and would have the name of the church on their nametapes with the Company name. A Company would have a close relationship with the church, and girls would attend services and church parades. At Guide Meetings there would be closing prayers and the singing of Guide 'Taps', itself a prayer.

For many girls before the Second World War their only holidays would be the occasional choir outing to the seaside and Guide camps were a welcome break.

One of the major attractions in joining the Girl Guides would have been the opportunity to make friends and as time went on to meet girls from other countries. In 1950 the 13th World Conference was held at Oxford and Guides and Brownies throughout the country prepared Friendship Scrolls to be given to the delegates from many lands. They were challenged to carry these across the country by different means, varying from on foot to by horse, boat or canoe! Scrapbooks were often illustrated with the stages of the journey.

The International element of the Guide Association has always been attractive to its members and opportunities to meet girls from other countries have existed since the early days.

Chapter 8

The Fifth Guide Law
' A Guide is courteous'

Jill, Lone Guide - by Ethel Talbot

Ethel Mary Talbot was one of a large family born to Hugh Talbot and his wife, Margaret. Born on 26th May 1880 in Sutton Coldfield, she died during the Second World War on 26th May 1944, aged 64, in Hayward's Heath.

Her father had private means and left an Army Career after joining the Plymouth Brethren. As a family they had several moves and, along with her several sisters and one brother, she was brought up in a religious atmosphere and well educated.

As an adult she left the Plymouth Brethren and later lived in Edinburgh and London, at one time teaching.

She evidently believed in the true worth of Guiding and wrote many books for schoolgirls on the subject, going from Brownies to Guides and Sea Rangers.

She is considered one of the major authors of schoolgirl stories.

This book was published in 1927 by Pearson, but my copy looks to date from the nineteen fifties, and is in the Mayflower Series published by Ward Lock and Company Ltd.

The dictionary definition of 'courteous' is 'polite, considerate or respectful in manner and action, obliging.' In the context of the Guide Law a Guide is expected to be polite to all, but especially to older people or those disadvantaged, and she must not take any reward for being helpful or courteous.

The book tells the story of Jill, beginning with Jill and her older brother, Harry, preparing to leave the home of their Aunt Agatha after her death. They are to leave Columbine Villa and Harry, an engineer, has found them rooms, where Jill can housekeep for them. A letter arrives from their aunt's cousin, Deborah Barrett, who has seen the announcement of Aunt Agatha's death, and now offers Jill a home with her. Jill does not want to accept, wanting to stay with Harry, and the move will be nearer Harry's work. Also she has had to cycle six miles to school and back and this has meant she is unable to join a troop of Guides. She has been Guiding on her own, as a Lone Guide.

Harry is engaged to Ethne and they are waiting for him to have a rise in salary, so that they can be married. Jill overhears them discussing that Harry has his rise already and Ethne wants to be married at once. However Harry wants to provide a home for Jill in

The dustwrapper shows Jill and her cat, Diddums

the small rooms they have taken. Jill sees how she can help them and writes to Aunt Deborah to accept her kind offer, also writing a letter to Harry telling him of this and that she hopes to take a Cookery Course. I think in this instance she is courteous and puts the needs of others first.

She leaves early next morning, taking with her Diddums, her cat, and going by train, changing trains to go to Midsum. She has to wait for two hours and goes to the waiting room, where a tired looking mother is trying to stop her baby crying. She snaps at Jill, but is then relieved when the sight of Diddums, the cat, distracts her baby. The mother tells her that since her husband died, she has had to go back into service, but although the last employer accepted the baby with her, the crying of the baby made her complain. The mother, Mrs Baker, then has walked out of the job and has now answered an advert for a job in Gilchester. She can take a kitchen maid with her and offers Jill the job, which Jill cannot take as she is going to her aunt's cousin at The Grange. She takes note of the address – 69, Hill Street, Gilchester, and is asked to call if out that way.

Jill walks to The Grange and learns that Miss Barrett has died suddenly, so returns to the railway station, planning to go back to Harry. As she hasn't enough money to do this she has enough to buy a ticket to Gilchester, planning to take up Mrs Baker's offer of a job.

She writes to Harry giving her new address and to say she hopes to learn to cook properly. Carrying her cat she arrives at Gilchester and asks for directions to 69 Hill Street, but while making her way there she is lost in the fog, then the cat runs off! She is glad to hear a voice in the fog, then manages to catch the cat, but when it escapes again, she loses contact with the voice. Having caught the cat again she tries to keep cheerful and decides to sleep in a doorway:

> Jill suddenly sat up. For an idea had come to her. Here, in the fog, so dreadfully alone, feeling unable, even, to think of Harry and Columbine Villa, for fear of breaking down, keeping her courage to the sticking point with all her might and main, the remembrance of Guides had somehow seemed like a spar to a drowning man. Jill had always been a Lone Guide, but a Lone Guide isn't a lonesome person; she had always seemed friendly with every other Guide all over the World.
>
> "And we're friends still. Having been only a Lone Guide makes that .... easier," thought Jill. " Suppose I sing ...... 'Taps', and imagine that I'm in the middle of a patrol and that all the rest are singing too!"

So she sings in the fog until some of the loneliness leaves her and she falls asleep.

When she wakes up she hears someone in trouble calling out and goes down to a basement to a frightened boy, Johnny, who tells her that his sister, Nance, is ill.

In the basement apartment, poorly furnished, a girl of her own age is ill, but refuses help, not wanting to take charity. Jill takes charge when she hears that despite being ill Nance has gone out to take sewing back to an employer. She insists on staying till morning to care for Nancy and will then find a doctor. In the meantime she makes a cup of tea and a poultice for the girl's chest:

It felt glorious, somehow to be doing something for somebody again; and to see puss curled on the rag rug before the little slacked-up fire. Quite unconsciously, Jill, bustling round to fill the kettle from a sink whose dripping tap had informed her of its whereabouts, suddenly remembered how as a Lone Guide she had longed for such an experience, though never had she guessed that it would come to her this way.

Thinking of the Guides who, in her imagination, rally round her she again sings " Taps" quietly and, to her surprise, Nancy opens her eyes and her eyes fill with joy. She tells Jill she won't turn out anyone who can sing that song!

Jill stays for a few days and the Doctor who comes is complimentary about her nursing. Nancy has some sewing to do for money and Jill helps her and sends Johnny to school. She discovers that although Nancy is not a Guide, she has happy memories of some Sea Guides who had their 'Ship' in a basement room let by her aunt and she had heard them sing " Taps". Her mother died when Johnny was born, then they were cared for by their mother's aunt, Aunt Teaser, who died a year ago. Nancy has taken over her job of keeping the wardrobes (costumes) from a Theatre, in good order, as she sews well. She has another job cleaning steps and has been able to rent the basement apartment. She mentions a friend, Jim, and her sister, Edie, who thinks Johnny should be in a Home and Nancy doesn't want this to happen.

The surroundings she is now in are evidently very poor but Jill fits in with ease and courtesy and takes the mended clothes back to Miss Buff at the Theatre.

She examines them and is satisfied and pays Jill, saying how highly she thinks of Nancy.

This is the first chance Jill has had to deal with her own business and she goes to find Mrs Baker at the Hill Street address, finding that it is a boarding house. A maid, Gladys, answers the door to her but rudely closes it when she hears that Jill is looking for Mrs Baker. Miss Sharp, the owner, calls her in telling her that Mrs Baker stayed only for one night, leaving her in the lurch. She is cross when Jill asks if a letter has arrived for her addressed to Miss Gillian Burke and Jill has to leave, but remains polite. Gladys follows her saying she is leaving her job shortly and gives Jill a letter, which has arrived for her, which Miss Sharp has told her to return to the postman. Jill offers to do something for Gladys and takes a message to her chap, who sells apples from a barrow.

There are two letters in the envelope, from Harry and Ethne, who both believe she has somewhere to live and a place at a Cookery School they know to be in the area, having misunderstood her letter.

Jill returns to Nancy, meeting the doctor leaving, and finds Nancy upset as her sister, Edie, has called and decided she will take Nancy and Johnny to her home the next day. Nancy doesn't want to lose her home and tells her about her friend, Jim, who has gone to be a sailor. He wants her to make a home with him, but when he was last home Nancy's aunt needed her and Nancy said she couldn't marry him yet. He has gone away and she hasn't seen him since then. The Sea Guides' singing of " Taps" has brought her comfort.

Nancy and her brother leave the next day, Jill sees them off and then tries to persuade the apartment owners to keep it for Nancy. They are unhelpful as they can soon find a new tenant. Jill is now on her own again, apart from her cat, and goes to the Cookery School as she thinks this will give her training and a place to live. She finds out that she needs to pay fees and so cannot go, but the Principal, Miss Gregory, suggests she goes to Mrs Hosker's office on Pitt Street, an employment agency.

When Jill arrives at the Agency she hears Miss Sharp, from 69 Hill Street, scolding the Agency Secretary over the girls sent to her as servants.

Jill overhears and knows that the maid, Gladys, will have left and that Harry and Ethne think she is living at 69 Hill Street. As she needs the job she speaks politely to Miss Sharp, offering to help until a proper maid is found.

Miss Sharp is desperate for help and accepts Jill's offer and, after she has left, the Agency secretary warns Jill that the work will be hard.

Jill can now write to Harry to say she has a proper job and does so. She starts work at the boarding house, where there are three groups of boarders, the Dining-rooms, the Drawing-rooms and the Top Floors, these being business people and out all day. She meets the Misses Druitt, whose requests have been overlooked before and is polite and helpful to them.

There is one other maid, Beattie, who avoids work as much as possible and often goes into the room of one of the Top Floor boarders, Mrs Montague, a milliner, preening herself in the mirror there.

Jill works very hard and, even after her afternoon off, when she usually stays in her room with Diddums, the cat, she finds that Beattie has neglected everything and she must put things tidy:

"Catch me doing anything for anyone," seemed Beattie's maxim. " It doesn't pay."

Miss Sharp is pleased with Jill and praises her:

" You're the best girl I've had for a whole year, Jill." said Miss Sharp, when Jill found time somehow to relieve her mistress of certain cooking chores. " I seem to get along somehow, now, and that's something. Here, don't stand about, get those clothes in to soak. We've no time for sitting round with our hands before us, and Beattie never is anywhere around when she's wanted."
Even that small grain of appreciation heartened Jill up for a whole day.

Jill has had letters from Nancy, who wants to see her, as she is not very happy, and she plans to go on a visit when she has been paid.

Mrs Montague reports the loss of a valuable pendant from her room and, at first, Jill is blamed, but then Beattie finds it on the stairs. Jill knows that Beattie must have stolen it, but she is still under suspicion herself and decides to leave. She packs her case and, carrying the cat, goes downstairs feeling angry and this is made worse when she hears Beattie singing and Mrs Montague playing her piano, as if nothing has happened.

Jill decides to walk the eight miles to see Nance, and the quietness as she walks into the countryside helps her to calm down. Her cat is hungry and two passing girls stop and give the cat a drink, despite Jill having no money. They have noticed that she is a Guide and one of them wears a badge herself and tells Jill she is nearly half way to her destination and to keep smiling:

But there had been a something in the very meeting of them that had done Jill good. " Keep smiling" – the very slogan meant something. After all, she had not shown herself as a Guide, really, by turning tail and leaving the house because she had been treated unjustly. They would think all the more for that, that Jill, a Guide, must have done what they thought she had done.

"And even if not … " decided Jill, pulling up suddenly beside the halfway milestone as she reached it, " it was running away from Duty. I think."

She is sure the way back seems shorter and that the whole invisible company of Guides seems to somehow keep pace with her. She is determined to see the job through as they can't manage without her. She will stick to it and pull it off!

It is seven o'clock when she reaches the door of Miss Sharp's boarding house and rings the area bell, She knows that she has fought a battle with herself and been victorious and, although there may be further battles, she will win those too.

Beattie opens the door, rather shamefaced, and greets her with the news that Miss Sharp, who has been acting as cook, is feeling unwell. She says it is just as well Jill has come back early:

- "Because I'm not going to start cooking dinners, not for anyone, and so I tell you. I've not come here as cook. Nor kitchen-maid, neither, as I said to Madam an hour ago. And that's that."

Jill tells Beattie that she should be ashamed of herself and goes to see Miss Sharp and, when the doctor arrives, he recognises her as the girl who nursed Nancy Teaser. Beattie has been paid and says she is leaving as boarders are going down with flu and she isn't going to help. Jill is once more polite and helpful to those who are ill and helps Beattie, when she feels unwell. Mr Montague, who is still well, helps Jill and tries to find some help from the Work Agency.

Gladys, who met Jill when she first came to the door of 69 Hill Street, comes to enquire how Miss Sharp is. She is to be married soon to her boyfriend, who now has a shop, but offers help for a while. This is a great help, but then Jill collapses and the doctor says she must have a rest and a day in the open air.

Jill decides to go to see Nance and sends a letter to her.

When she arrives at Edie's, where Nance is staying, Edie says that Johnny is a handful but a friend is willing to look after him. Edie's husband will pay for this and Jill meets the friend, Mary Budger, and thinks that Johnny will be lucky to board there. To her surprise Mrs Baker, the mother she met on the train when she left home, is there with her baby, the child being cared for by Mary Budger. She tells Jill about the house in Phillimore Gardens, where she worked before her marriage and the ladies there who had been sad when she left.

Nance is glad to see Jill, but is pining for her lost friend, Jim.

Jill travels back to her job, calling at the Theatre, to see if Miss Buff will let Nance do some sewing again and meets a sailor. He is asking about the shop called 'Teaser's' and asks Jill if she knows the people there, including a young boy, and a girl called Nance. Jill realises this is Nance's Jim and sees him off on the train to Oasebrook to see Nance. At 69 Hill Street Gladys greets her with the news that Miss Sharp is to retire and, when Jill goes to see her, she is retiring on health grounds. She apologises for not trusting Jill, as Beattie has told her the truth before leaving and she is concerned about the Misses Druitt. Jill suggests to the Misses Druitt that they can take over the 10 years left on the lease of the boarding house for their own use and, as they talk, realises that they are the former employers of Mrs Baker. She thinks she can invite Mrs Baker to work for them again.

Gladys and Jill have a chat and Jill says that she would like to go to the Cookery College, but can't. Her brother, Harry, arrives at the same time as the doctor, who has told him that Jill is running 69 Hill Street. When she fainted it was the doctor's son who came to see her, and he realises that Jill is the girl from the foggy evening, whom he had helped to find her cat. Unfortunately he had hurt his ankle in a fall and lost contact with her. His was the voice in the fog!

Jill tells Harry all that has happened and Harry is pleased to say that Aunt Deborah has left her a legacy. She can now afford to go to the Cookery College and the doctor says that the principal, Miss Gregory, is a friend and Jill can make the doctor's house her second home. He invites them to go round right away and Jill is overwhelmed, but very happy.

Fact or Fiction ?

I am sure that Guides at the time this book was written in 1927 were very aware of the Law regarding being courteous or polite. At that time girls were brought up to be respectful to all adults, whether their parents, friends of their parents, (often called Aunty and Uncle), teachers, employers and quite naturally their Guide Leaders. Early Guiders were quite often single ladies from good families who did not need to work for their living and chose Guiding as an outlet for their energies and to make a difference to the lives of generations of girls.

A Guide would quite naturally be courteous, realising that her behaviour would be judged as that of all Guides. How easy it would have been (and still is) to slip from this behaviour, and how hard many girls must have tried.

Like Judy in the story they would feel it was part of Guiding to put others' needs before your own and to be polite and courteous in doing so.

One of my Guide friends always says that miserable adults were miserable young people, and maybe, in the same way, courteous older folk were courteous in their youth. In my own experience of contact with former Guiders and Trefoil Guild Members (mainly retired Guide people), these ladies have been invariably courteous and interested in my projects as a Guide Archivist. I have no doubts that they as Guides in the 1920's and 1930's were the same.

My own mother, Eva Oseman (nee George), was involved in Guiding from about 1926, at the age of 13, to 1939, as Guide then Ranger and Ranger Guider. She was brought up by her paternal grandparents, having lost both parents in the Spanish Flu epidemic in 1919. She was as an adult polite and courteous – even taking this to extremes and never putting herself forward, preferring to work in the background. Asked to run a cake stall at a village event she set to and produced a fine display, only for it to be handed over to a more outgoing lady on the day. She made no protest but simply went to help someone else.

When I began to research local Guiding in 1996 I visited a number of elderly ladies who had been Guides at the time of 'Jill, Lone Guide.'

There was Dorothy Hinton, who ran the 1st Malvern Link Brownies for

42 years from 1938 to 1980. Her Guiding began in 1930 as a Guide for a month, then a Ranger and Guider. Forthright and amusing she was happy to share her memories and we met to do so several times. Another was Margaret Grundy, a Ranger in 1935 in 12th Malvern Rangers with Dorothy and previous to this a Guide in 14th Malvern Guides. Tall and energetic she was a friend of my parents and had appeared several times at my Guide Company's camps, helping Captain. She had worked as a nurse, social worker, and personnel officer in Wartime and as Warden of a Mother and Baby Home, then in the Canadian Sunday School Mission and again later in social work. She had kept up her Guiding, running Ranger Units and in retirement lived in a lovely old house, used as a Professional Women's Club. Well educated and charming she was always welcoming.

Also living in the same place was Phyllis Castle, educated at Malvern Girls' College, a Guide there and, having left school in 1925/1926 returned to her family home in Cheltenham. Not wishing to sit and knit, as friends did at their get-togethers, she ran a Brownie Pack, then was a Guide Lieutenant and was persuaded in Wartime to open a new Sea Ranger Unit in landlocked Cheltenham.

12th Malvern Ranger Company, 1935

She spent many years working for the WRVS, including time as welfare officer for a Ghurka Regiment. Gently spoken and charming she gave us afternoon tea and biscuits, as did Miss Mollie Crofts, once my school Needlework Teacher. Prior to Miss Croft's move to live near her niece she sorted out her Guide Memorabilia for our Archives and treated us to afternoon tea with a trolley of food and tray cloths and bone china.

Finally I would include Jean Milward, my Guide and Ranger Captain and also my mother's Guide Captain for a time, friend, mentor and engaging companion. In her last years I visited often, always received with the same warm welcome and encouragement to 'tell me all the news!' She treated everyone the same, from farmer at Guide Camp to Lady Baden-Powell, our Chief Guide, and made time for all her 'girls'.

These are a few only of those I am proud to have known and there are more, still blessedly with us, continuing their Guiding as Trefoil Guild Members. They are unfailingly helpful and 'go the extra mile' whenever they can.

Chapter 9

The Sixth Guide Law
'A Guide is a Friend to Animals'

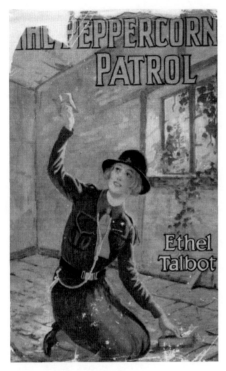

The Peppercorn Patrol - by Ethel Talbot

The book, the'Peppercorn Patrol', was issued by Cassell in 1929, and my first edition was given to Gladys Morris on July 15th 1931.

At the beginning of the story Peggy Parry and her younger sisters, twins Jack and Jill (Jacqueline and Gillian), are travelling by train to a very 'out-of-the –way back of beyondish spot'. They are boarders at St Brenda's, 'a topping school', where they are considered as 'good sports all! Good at Games; good at Guides; good at Work; good all round.'

School has broken up early because of a scarlet fever scare, closing midway through July, losing nearly a quarter of the summer term.

As their parents are abroad, they generally go home to Aunt Teresa, but this time she is afraid they will pass scarlet fever to her own small children. Peggy and Jill have had this already, but Jack has not, so Aunt Teresa is willing to take the two but wants to arrange something else for Jack. The sisters opt to stay together and are sent to stay with a Mrs Wallace, their aunt's housekeeper's sister. She lives in the country at Mossmoore, a quiet spot.

Peggy is now a Ranger and Jack and Jill Guides and members of the Hollyhock Patrol and, although they will miss the sports and swimming at school, hope to be able to concentrate on their Guiding. They will have plenty of time and the countryside around them:

For there were such heaps of topping Guidish things they could do, wherever they found themselves. And the "Back-of- Beyond" – to which the slow train seemed to be taking them – would be specially good for certain Guiding ploys.

"The lonelier the better. I say, was that a heron's note … or a foghorn?" inquired Jill. "I'll get some fine new birds here, I rather think, and make the Hollyhocks stare."

Jill was working for her naturalist badge, Jack, whose idea of one holiday occupation at least is to secure the photographer's badge, chimed in.

" Jolly good. We'll work together. With my vest-pocket camera, you know. We'll find them out and then snap them unbeknownst. We might get to know a topping lot about birds in this quarter, I rather think."

When they alight at the station at Mossmoore a solitary porter stares incredulously at their baggage, as they have brought cameras, a gramophone, billycans, and haversacks. Jill's Guide hat, signalling flags and a small Union Jack! They don't feel this to be unusual!

They are taken from the station on a cart a lad has driven in with milk and receive a not very friendly reception at the New Dower House from Mrs Wallace. She is not used to girls of their age and is amazed that they have brought so much luggage with them, but lets them in.

She is shocked too that they aim to wear their Guide Uniforms and has never heard of Guides. She is also going to place a lot of restrictions on them.

They nickname her 'Mrs Gummidge', as she is a glum sort of person, but they remain polite and find some excuse for her behaviour as she shortly will have to leave her home. She has been allowed to live there by the Major from the Manor, but he too will have to leave his home quite soon.

Mrs Wallace feeds them well but she is unhappy about the quantity of their belongings and does not want to house their Guide Collections – wild flowers and so on:

"Wild flowers! In here! Why, everyone knows they're nothing better than weeds. Collecting! Why, that's right-down crazy, and untidy too!"

The girls want to find somewhere to put their belongings and use as a 'clubroom' and go out to find somewhere, stumbling on a track leading to a neglected house.

Exploring inside they find that although it is part derelict, there will be rooms they can use. Looking around, they find dead flowers thrown on the floor and three nests in the chimney corner.

Jill thinks it is like a fairy-place with birds nesting, but Peggy knows differently:

Three nests were there – empty, deserted; but once formed with loving care by parent birds.

Peggy stepped across and shook her head.

"You're wrong about that, Jill. These weren't built here. This is a robin's nest; this one's a water wagtail's. I'm horribly afraid that the person who tore up the flowers …… tore off these, too."

"Oh, dear, and I'd thought …"

It had been such a topping thought, and the realisation of what must certainly be the truth, had wakened Jill from what had seemed such a house of dreams. The little deserted house had seemed so beautiful – till now. Broken egg-shells, stamped into the stone floor of the kitchen on which they stood, went to prove that mischief, alone, had been responsible for this part of their find.

They go on to find the attic inhabited by swallows, the tiles of the roof being broken allowing them to fly in and out freely:

Here, indeed, were nests – generations probably of swallow's nests.

" Oh! Oh! Oh! It isn't an attic at all. It's …… a birdery!" called Jill.

100

This brings back the magic of the cottage for her and she places the nests in a corner of the beams, hoping they will be used.

They light a fire in the hearth downstairs and tidy up and are interrupted by two small girls, who want their 'nestses back.'

Although Jack is cross with them for taking the nests, they are attracted to Jill who speaks kindly to them:

"Yes, lady. 'Ou can 'ave 'em, lady, if you want 'em."

"But the birds want them most." Jill's tone was troubled. " I couldn't possibly want them. There would have been baby birds there, if you'd left the nests in the trees."

"Oh, there was, lady!" Two excited chatterers burst out into eager reminiscences. "Oh, there was! We brung 'em down, but we flung 'em into the bushes. It were the nestses as were pretty."

"But…" Peggy stood quite still, so did Jack. Jill, however, spoke to the quaint little pair who faced her, eagerly explaining the cruelty of their ignorance. "Oh, how could you? To kill them!"

"Why, bless you lady!" There was a hint of superior pity in the voice of the child who spoke – "birds can't feel."

Jack is disgusted and Jill hesitates to speak, but the children shout at Jack, who turns to go upstairs. The children reveal that they are afraid of the 'spooks' up there, They are half Romany children and are travelling folk, cared for by their Romany grandfather and their dad, who is a 'mumper' as they are, a name for travellers. Their names are Bina and Lobelia and they have laid a trail to the cottage called a 'patrin' using wild flowers, which of course have died.

They are taken up to the attic to see the birds after being told there are no 'spooks' up there.

Jill tells them that they are swallows and as it is July most of the little birds have learned to fly, but some are still practising. The children ask if there are 'nestses' there. Peggy waits for Jill's reply:

Jill was so fond of small weak things: all her life she had been like that, and Guiding had appealed so strongly to that side of her. And Jill had been heartbroken at the havoc that these very children had

101

wrought – by want of thought rather than by want of heart – that Peggy wondered what her younger sister would say.

But Jill said the right thing. "Yes, there are nests up there – that's part of the loveliness. They made the nests in time for the eggs, you know, and the baby birds were born there. And they were safe there because …… nobody wanted to harm them, and so the baby birds grew up to learn to fly."

"Oh, lady!" There was a mixture of expressions in the children's faces. Cute little things that they were, already they began to see the drift of Jill's words.

She goes on to tell them how happy these birds were but there were other nests not so happy – those they had taken. She offers to show them the birds and they go with her and think the birds sweet. They promise never to touch any nests again.

When they all leave the cottage Bina points out the flowers they had picked and used to mark the way – they had been pretty but were now dead. Peggy asks what their grandfather uses for a 'patrin' and the children said he would use bits of willow. Jack says that she is sure their grandfather, a true Romany, wouldn't use wild flowers that would die and the children agree. They part to go home.

'Mrs Gummidge' has been busy tidying up their bedrooms and, as they sit over a hot supper, they learn that the house they have found is the Old Dower House, the original dower house. She also tells them more about the Major and the Manor House. They notice lights in three windows of the Manor House.

The next day is to be their 'Flitting Day' when they take their Guiding equipment to the Old Dower House, despite 'Mrs Gummidge's' misgivings.

They fit up their clubroom, hoist the Union Jack and feel very happy about it. They hear someone shouting "COO-E-E-E-E-E!" and meet two girls who are wearing Tenderfoot badges like their own Guide badges, finding out that they are Australian and the granddaughters of the Major. 'Mrs Gummidge' enjoys telling her visitors about their father, Master Basil, the Major's son.

The three are invited to lunch at the Manor House so that they can all talk about Guide matters and they learn more about the history of the estate and why a family called 'Sartin' are trying to claim the Manor and estate.

The Major tells them that the 'Old' Dower House was built for his great grandmother, Dame Muriel, after her son had married, and that she liked the view from it of the Manor House. When her daughter-in-law needed a dower house herself the New Dower House was built for her.

It is likely that he will have to move from the Manor (and Mrs Wallace from her house), as he is unable to prove the property is his own. The Major is happy to let the Parrys and his grand-daughters use the Old Dower House for a peppercorn lease and they decide that as they will all be doing Guide work there they will be the Peppercorn Patrol.

The Australian girls, Poppy and Jan Dacre, tell them that they are trying to find the lost deeds to the Manor.

When the five girls visit the Old Dower House they find their clubroom in a muddle and their Union Jack missing. They suspect that Bina and 'Belia have done this and plan to follow their 'patrin', their tracks and find them. However they find the two children up in the attic, watching the swallows and their young, and they are dressed up in the Union Jack and some signalling flags:

> Their cute little faces wore expressions so child-like, innocent and – wonderstruck, as they gazed at the birds above, that suddenly the truth seemed plain.
>
> Jill had been right. Peggy had, for a moment, wondered whether her younger sister should have brought these two into the secret of the birdery, but... Jill had been right.
>
> As Peggy was realizing that, suddenly the little pair rose.
>
> The birds did not seem to be afraid of them as, together, they threw out their arms in imitation of the whirring wings above and executed a bird-dance as simple as it was sweet.
>
> Then, turning, they saw the watchers at the door.
>
> Their eyes glowed, their smiles came and went with welcome. Still 'flying,' unhampered by the draperies, they flitted across the floor.
>
> "S-s-s-sh!" whispered 'Belia. "They is so sweet! Like the lady said."

"You'd better not fwighten them," whispered Bina. "'Course they doesn't mind us, but you has to sit very still."

The girls make up the Peppercorn Patrol, consisting of one Ranger, four Guides, and two Brownies-in-the-making. They teach Bina and 'Belia about Guides and they grasp the knowledge very quickly.

The five older girls have an overnight camp, which they keep secret from the little girls. While sitting over a campfire they hear a bell ringing and wonder what it is.

Bina and 'Belia are learning to do lots of Brownie and Guide activities and Jill tells them about their camp and that they have been on the bog-land looking for the sundew plant without success:

> She was working for the Bird-Lover's badge now, as well as for the Naturalist's. The birds had grown to be a big interest here, in this out-of-the –way spot. The work for the Naturalist's badge was almost done: her coloured drawings of nineteen flowers – specimens she had collected- were finished, and their descriptions were carefully written down. The twentieth, which completed the number, must be sundew, so Jill had decided long ago.

The holidays are going by quickly and in September the little girls will be moving on, the Parrys going back to school and the Dacres will go back to Australia, without having been able to help their grandfather to prove his claim to the Manor and estate.

The Major suggests they have a proper supper camp to mark the end of the holiday and, while this is taking place, they are woken by Bina and 'Belia's grandfather as the children have gone missing. He is grateful for their care of the children and now, while he and their father have been away at a fair, the two girls have disappeared. They have been 'flitsome' for the past week, saying they have 'summot for to do at night-time', which he has told them not to do.

Jill remembers the girls have been whispering about a 'secret' and guesses that they may have gone into the bog where the sundew is, so Peggy sends their grandfather back to his camp after he gives her directions onto the bog.

As they reach it they hear a cry and meet two Sea-Rangers, who have helped Bina and 'Belia out of the bog where 'Belia has found the sundew for Jill. They take the pair back to the Sea-Ranger camp a mile or so away and Peggy goes back to tell the grandfather.

Mrs Wallace and the Sea-Rangers are invited to the 'Old Dower House' the next day and the Dacres and Parrys prepare for the visit. When they go upstairs to see the two small girls dancing, a plank comes loose, falling into the Guide room and a small metal case is dislodged. This contains the missing documents, which confirm the Major's right to the Manor and estate, so everyone can be happy and both the Major and Mrs Wallace can stay in their homes.

Fact or Fiction ?

This is a quickly moving story which, although sentimental, stresses the love of a Guide for birds and flowers and that she is keen to pass this on to others.

Collecting and pressing flowers would have been a common pastime for girls of that age whether Guides or not and recognising the various birds and their eggs appealed to many girls. Taking the appropriate badges would have been a way of furthering this interest.

Pictures are from a logbook kept by the Silver Birch Patrol in 1927.
They have kept their colours after eighty years.

105

At the Guide Training House, Foxlease, in the New Forest there are logbooks kept from the 1920's by Guiders on trainings there. Those from the earlier dates contain the most beautiful sketches of flowers and birds, many of these young women having received the benefit of drawing and painting lessons.

Many girls today are not 'into' collecting but for children of the 1930's up to the 1960's it was normal to have a number of collections from stamps, coins, cigarette and tea cards to pressed flowers.

It was also normal for girls living in the country to be able to recognise the various birds, some of which regrettably are now comparatively rare.

Most girls would have a pet of some sort, from a goldfish or budgerigar or canary to a cat or dog, this being in an age when there were not so many heavily built-up areas or heavy traffic.

Along with the promise to do your duty to God is the realisation that part of this consists of respect for the world around us, respect for animals, birds, plants and the whole of creation.

Chapter 10

The Seventh Guide Law
'A Guide Obeys Orders'

Sea Rangers at Sloo - by Geoffrey Prout

Blackie published this book in 1949, and I may well have the first edition, my copy having been produced to 'Book Production War Economy Standard.'

My copy has a bookplate of a monk and the words 'Ex Libris Saint Bernard's Convent High School.' The foreword is by Ailne F. Nicholl, Essex County Sea Ranger Coxswain, and dated 23rd April 1948 and reads:

> Mr. Prout has written Sea Rangers at Sloo primarily as a story of the activities of the Sea Ranger Ship Reliance, but his description of the wild life of the Essex creeks and marshlands, and the local customs, will appeal to many "not-so-young" readers, as well as those for whom the book is intended.
>
> Although not many Sea Ranger Crews will achieve such an adventurous career, they could all with advantage aim at being able to deal with the emergencies which fall to the lot of S.R.S. Reliance and therefore, on behalf of Essex Sea Rangers, I wish Mr. Prout every success with his very excellent yarn.

Early explanation of this Law says that for Guides obedience must not be for fear of punishment, but in every sense of the word. For a Guide this will mean obeying the orders of her Patrol Leader and of her Captain, and obeying the rules of the Guide Movement. For a member of the Army this would translate as Discipline.

In this book the obedience of rules relates to the special rules to do with rivers and the sea. For Sea Rangers obedience was needed both for the 'Crew' to work together and for their own safety and that of others.

The story is that of Monica Wilburton and her cousins, Tess and Joan, who are sent to East Anglia for the school holidays, travelling to a place in Essex, called Sloo.

Arriving at Withinghoe Station, they find no one has come to meet them, but a Sea Ranger group leaving the same train catches their attention. They wait outside the ticket office until a message is passed on to them, telling them that Tom Hathaway, who is meant to meet them, has had a motor breakdown. They are to go to Sloo Manor by bus, where they will be staying with Miss Grimthorpe. The Sea Rangers offer to take them with them, crossing the estuary by boat, and the three accept the offer to go on the motor launch, Sea Queen.

The Sea Rangers efficiently load all their equipment onto a truck and Monica, Tess and Joan help to push the loaded truck from the station and to load the gear onto the boat.

The Sea Rangers are friendly and the three cousins watch all the action with the keenest interest. The Skipper is free to talk to and watch them as the Bo 'sun, Carol Graham, takes charge:

The Bo 'sun wasn't saying much either. Indeed all she said was "Take Bowman, June. Sandra, go aft and stand by."

June clambered over the stowed gear and stood on the fore platform of the launch and took a couple of turns of the head-rope off the cleat. Sandra, who had first suggested that the friends should cross over to Sloo with the Rangers, came aft, stood up on the stern-bench, using Joan's shoulder without permission as an additional aid in heaving herself up, and put her hand on the stern rope. She too took a couple of turns of the cleat, and held the slack end of the rope ready. Both June and Sandra now looked at the torpedo-bearded captain, who was wiping his hands on some cotton waste as he walked from the engine towards the wheel.

"All right," he said, "let go, bow."

June threw the end of her rope ashore and then pulled on the standing part, and the rope snaked through the big iron ring on the quayside.

"All gone for'ard!" she cried in a ringing voice.

The captain smiled and nodded approvingly.

"I'd like it if *all* my passengers was *always* Sea Rangers," grinned the captain as he opened the throttle.

They are soon rounding the beacon to head up Sloo Channel and the captain is preparing to cast the lead to take soundings (of the water depth) and asks for one of the Sea Rangers to steer. The Ranger skipper suggests it will be good practice for the Rangers to do it all themselves, to which the captain agrees.

Three Rangers converged on the wheel, and there was just the suspicion of a struggle, till Skipper said sharply:
"None of that! Mavis, you take the wheel first. You'd better sound, Hilary, and you watch her and instruct, Carol."

These orders are instantly obeyed.

Tess, Joan and Monica help with off loading the equipment and they are to stay at the Manor while Monica's father is 'attending something military abroad'. Tess and Joan's parents are in Africa, so they live with Monica in the holidays from Millverne Girls' College in Worcestershire.

The Sea Rangers, obeying their skipper, Miss Cheyney, check out their equipment and prepare to carry it to their campsite, near Sloo Manor. The three girls help by carrying the peg-bags with their free hands, their cases in the other hands, following Skipper's orders. Near the Manor they thank the skipper for the lift in the boat and leave the Sea Rangers to go onto their field site.

Arriving at the Manor, they ring the bell and are met by an elderly lady, who introduces herself as Miss Grimthorpe. She is an old friend of both fathers, General and George Wilburton, and they are to call her Auntie Grim! She tells them about the Sea Rangers and Sloo Manor and also that she attended the same school as the girls.

The house is old, but there is a modern bathroom and plenty of hot water, so they hurry to tidy up after the journey and go downstairs for tea. They tell her about the trip over on the boat and enjoy their tea. Auntie Grim tells them about a 'lazy good-for-nothing', Sam Borrowdene, who helps the Sea Rangers, but is a bit of a rogue. He lives on an old houseboat nearby. She also mentions that Bill Gooding, her cowman and farm manager has to close the 'Sloo', this time a sluice that lets water in and out.

The girls explore the Manor grounds, which include five square yards of tessellated pavement recently uncovered. Deciding to go to the Sea Rangers' camp, at the gate they meet a man in an old tweed jacket, corduroy trousers, long boots and a floppy tweed shooting-hat. He is Sam Borrowdene, who has been to sell some fish to the Sea Rangers. The girls are not very friendly and he takes himself off. The Sea Rangers point out Sam's houseboat and say that he keeps a sort of unofficial 'Watch of the Wardstaff' over the saltings. This has proved very useful on more than one occasion.

Returning to the Manor the girls look at family photos, then go to bed.

The next day Tess, Joan and Monica sleep in and, after breakfast, go out to look around the farm, meeting Mr Goodey and his Labrador, Rhapsody. After lunch they are to meet the girl from the local post office, who is coming to visit. She is seventeen years old and works, having Thursday and Saturday free.

She arrives on her bike and is a very pretty girl, called Dagmar Freeman, and they show her round the farm, but she doesn't seem very interested. Dagmar keeps looking through the arched gateway with a view of the sea and she confesses that she has come hoping to meet the Sea Rangers.

They go over to the camp, arriving as a parade finishes, and are talking to Skipper when Sam Borrowdene rushes in to tell them that some children have been cut off by the tide at a place called Inner Horse. He needs the Sea Rangers' help as swimmers and they set off, running to the lower corner of the field.

Some of the girls are far ahead and Sam asks Miss Cheyney to call them back, as they will get stuck in the duckweed. Miss Cheyney orders:

"All Rangers keep close-to! Sam will tell us when to push ahead. Come back, June and Sandra, and you Wilburton girls! Keep in line!"

Tess, Joan and Monica obey and slow down along with Sandra, June and Dagmar, but some of the Rangers have already slipped off their skirts and shirts and are running ahead in bathing costumes, ready to swim.

The girls in front wade across Sloo Channel and then have to swim, but are trapped in the duckweed. The others follow Sam's instructions and his directions. Sam is sure the swimmers in the duckweed are safe, but asks the skipper to swim on with the best swimmers, as he cannot swim and the situation is now desperate. Miss Cheyney instructs the best swimmers to attempt the rescue, going up-tide to cross the channel or they will be swept away by the tide. They wade out, then swim and are much nearer the children and Tess, Joan, Monica, June and Dagmar reach them first. Following them are Sandra, Carol Graham and two other Sea Rangers and Miss Cheyney. They manage to save the children, who are very scared, and to get them back to land, although it is almost impossible to swim against the incoming tide. The Rangers caught in the duckweed also manage to get back and helpers meet the party and everyone is taken to Sloo Manor to get into dry clothes. Sam goes back to his houseboat, although Miss Grimthorpe presses him to come along:

> "No, Ma'am, my house-boat's close by," he said. "Bless you, ma'am I've been wet afore! T'isn't a new thing for me to get me boots full o' water an' drag along double-quick over them saltings bein' druv by the toyde. You'll hev enough commotion up at the manor wi'out me making the crowd bigger. Besides, I haven't done nothen. 'Twas those girls did all the work."
>
> "You did the thinking!" flashed out Monica.
>
> Sam Borrowdene guffawed.
>
> "Ah, I be powerful good at thinkin'," he said. "I've druv meself to sleep, thinkin', many's the toyme."

Tess, Joan and Monica are keen to join Sea Rangers and Auntie Grim agrees to talk to Miss Cheyney. She also tells them about the manor boat, which could have been used today if nearer to hand. It is certificated for sixteen Sea Rangers and she gives permission for the girls to use it 'but you must obey any bounds that rascal, Sam Borrowdene, lays down for you'.

They rush to the Sea Ranger camp to talk to them about the boat, which is known to them, and they too are eager to go out in it. June tells the Bo'sun that they are going to look at the boat, called a galley, with the Warburtons:

> "Righto!" came Carol's voice from another tent. "You're not to go out in the galley, you know."
>
> "No, I know!" called back June.

111

They borrow Sam's dinghy to go out to the boat, mess about in it, and then return to the Camp and Manor House. They find Miss Cheyney at the Manor House, and she agrees to the Wilburton girls and Dagmar becoming Sea Rangers. Auntie Grim explains how they will go to and from the meetings and Miss Cheyney talks to them:

> "You see, girls, becoming a Sea Ranger is a thing not to be taken lightly," smiled Skipper. "All of you to-day have proved that you are first-class swimmers and that you have a keen sense of public duty. There is a pre-enrolment test, and this requires regular attendance at weekly musters for three months. That'll mean travelling to my headquarters at Norrington."

She goes on to explain about attending the meetings called musters, about the Promise and Law and uniform:

> "Now there's one other thing you must consider seriously before you decide, and that is that you will be prepared to obey the Rules, for organisation and policy, and not depart from them on any account. I refer now particularly to the boat. The rules lay down that no Sea Ranger can take out a boat without holding a boating permit or charge certificate. None of you will be able to have one until after enrolment - at least three months - and then only if you can pass the test before such is granted. Now you know what that means. It means that you will not be able to use even your own boat no matter whether you have used it before or not. So, girls, you see that right at the outset becoming a Sea Ranger means giving up something. I know you would love to push off Sea Rangering in the manor boat on your own, and have no doubt set such plans for yourselves, since Miss Grimthorpe has told me that she has already given you permission to do so. I do not doubt that you could do so in perfect safety, but there you are! Those are the rules, and if you are to be Sea Rangers, you must obey them."

They want to be Sea Rangers so much that they agree to all this and not to mind not using the boat, which pleases Miss Cheyney. She says they can go out with herself, Carol, June and Sandra, all of whom have 'Charge

Certificates', or with Sam Borrowdene. They can also use the boat on their own while not actually taking part in Sea Ranger activities or wearing the uniform.

The next day the girls want to show Sandra from the Sea Rangers the tessellated pavement, but find she has already seen it. Instead they decide to use a ladder to look at the sundial on the brick archway at the Manor. They achieve this with some difficulty, due to the size of the ladder and how they have to manoeuvre it, and find that the sundial and its inscription are covered in verdigris. Joan fetches an old table knife to scrape this away and a notebook and pencil to write down the Latin inscription.

At lunch they ask Auntie Grim, who knows Latin from her schooldays, to translate this and it reads: "The custom of the manor and the place is to be observed. Custom is to be held as law." The date is 1603 and Auntie is surprised at their knowing the words on the sundial, and more so when she hears that they have been up a ladder! Joan later asks Tom Hathaway to help her to put the ladder up again, so that she can photograph the inscription.

When the Sea Rangers go out in the galley, taking the girls, Sam Borrowmere helps with the instructions and they have a good trip out rowing.

Orders are given and instantly obeyed. They also enjoy it when they can hoist the sails and take soundings.

On Sunday the Sea Rangers and the contingent from the Manor go to church and the vicar preaches a sermon about the rescue, praising the Sea Rangers and those from the Manor as they 'were prepared for service.'

The girls make the acquaintance of the horse 'Kitty' and have to catch her, then, Auntie Grim agrees they can ride her. The girls groom the horse and smarten her up.

Joan's photos of the sundial come out well, but they notice that a few of the letters in some of the words actually stand out.

The girls from the Manor and Dagmar join in with some camp activities and, as new recruits for S.R.S. Reliance, learn the Promise, Law, Salute and Flag. They accompany Skipper and the Sea Rangers to Withinghoe on the galley, obeying Skipper's orders:

"Mavis, Clare, Joan and Sandra will be the crew for the return trip, and will be passengers on the way over. The crew for the outward trip, of course, will be passengers on the way back. Dagmar, you will be passenger both ways, since you can't row. Now parade on the left of the crew, you passengers."

They all do as they are told and all the appropriate instructions and orders are given for letting go the mooring, bringing in fenders and so on.

At Withinghoe there is a shop selling Wrens' hats, so they do their shopping and return to the galley.

This has had to be moved because of the tide and on the way home the fog comes down. Skipper takes out her compass and, unfortunately, drops it overboard, so they have to work out their position from soundings and deduction, rowing in between. They then decide to drop anchor until the fog lifts and camp down in the bottom of the boat, taking watches. At one in the morning a wind arises and they can see a wreck buoy and then other lights and work out how to go in to Sloo Outfall. They row in satisfactorily to be met by Sam Borrowdene and some of the farm men. Miss Grimthorpe takes them all in for a hot meal and to dry their clothes.

Monica, Tess and Joan want Dagmar to ride the horse, Kitty, but she is reluctant to do so and some of the Sea Rangers try to ride, with little success at first. As goodnights are said and they walk back to the Manor, they are still suggesting Dagmar should ride. Some of the girls think that she is swanking and doesn't want to show herself up, but not all agree as Dagmar evidently can ride but chooses not to. Dagmar decides to ride after all and proceeds to give a display of circus riding. She is afraid they will think her just a common little circus girl and not want to be friends with her. She explains her circus background, being brought up by a lady she calls auntie after the death of her mother and her father's neglect. This lady has found her the job at the Post Office with her sister, Mrs Summer, as she has not wanted her to work in the circus. Auntie Grim already knows her background.

They now suspect that Kitty has been a circus horse as she behaves so well for Dagmar and Auntie Grim says she has been told the horse has come from circus stables.

They learn about the ceremony of the 'Watch of the Wardstaff', which dates back to Saxon days.

Sam Borrowdene takes the Sea Rangers and the Manor girls to look at white stones in the sea-wall, which he believes may be guiding marks for crossing the saltings and may be part of an old stone wharf. Trying to find the wharf, they find cockle-shell gravel, which Sam says is man-made, and this makes a sort of track.

When the Sea Rangers are in Joan and Tess's bedroom practising chart and compass work, June, looking out of the window, sees a white line across the cornfield leading to the white stones. They tell Auntie Grim about this line, which is seen when the wind ruffles the corn.

Joan later points out that the white line, continued, would lead to the archway with the sun-dial and inscription, and they look at her photos of the inscription. They see that the letters N S E C A P and L stand out. Tess suggests reading this backwards, when it will read L paces N, which they work out as fifty paces north!

They rush out to see and use a pick where the number of paces leads them to the back of the stables. They find some granite stones and Miss Grimthorpe decides she will have the men dig the rest of the way, and they find a flagstone over what seems to be a space. They fetch some lifting gear and Miss Grimthorpe says that Sir George Heaney from Braythewick Hall needs to be consulted, as he is writing a book about this part of Essex.

Once the flagstone is lifted a deep black cell is revealed with rusty iron rungs leading down. They fetch a stepladder to go down safely and Joan is allowed to go down after Tom, who finds a heavy square box. Some of the other men go down to help by securing ropes to bring the box to the surface.

They clean off the box which is

Finding the lead box and lifting it.
The Sea Rangers are helping the men.

115

inscribed with a Dutch name and the word 'Sluys' and the year 1603, but are disappointed to find that it contains only faded papers.

When Sir George arrives, he meets the girls and is fascinated by the ancient track and the wharf. He locks the box away safely in his car, while he is taken to see the discoveries.

Joan is still keen to know why the brick archway was built, but Sir George thinks it may have been for farm use, to gauge the height of hay on a wagon. He is more interested in the possibility of the track being on the site of an ancient Roman roadway.

The next excitement is when Dagmar arrives by bike the next morning and tells them that Sir George has been on the saltings since dawn. There is now no sign of him and the tide is coming in. She wants to find Sam Borrowdene to lead the rescue-party, and the Sea Rangers and local men are keen to make a line to search. When Dagmar returns at last with Sam, he works out from the movement of birds on the estuary where Sir George may be. He gives directions to the men, but then sees that the Sea Rangers understand better and tells the men to let them lead the way. He tells Miss Cheyney that they should take the boat out with the outboard motor, as the searchers may not be able to pull Sir George out of the mud, but can maybe keep his head above water until they reach him in the boat.

The land party walk over the saltings and find Sir George sunk in mud up to his chest. They crawl over the mud and manage to drag him out to where the men can take over. June and Sandra start resuscitation until they can get him onto the galley, which they do by dragging Sir George and June on a board and then onto the boat.

On the way back to land Carol takes over the resuscitation from June and, when they are near Sheldon Sand Beacon and can see the manor house, Hilary uses signal flags to send a message to someone on their camp. She first sends the attention sign and after a reply sends the message:

"Dr. Hills will need ambulance. Sir George apparently drowned. Artificial respiration now being applied." Hilary got the reception C's promptly, gave the Ac-R, rolled the flags and stood down.

Tom Hathaway, once a signaller in the army, tells the other men what the message is and they are impressed by the Sea Rangers' skills. They are afraid that Sir George is dead, but, although Carol hears, she continues the resuscitation until he is delivered to Dr. Hill and the ambulance. The rescuers all go back to welcoming Sloo Manor to clean up.

In the afternoon the message comes by phone to the Manor saying that Sir George is breathing and will pull through thanks to the Sea Rangers who did the resuscitation. This news is passed on to the farm men and to Sam Borrowdene and the Sea Rangers. The Sea Rangers return to their camp, needing to have an early night as they are to leave for home the next day.

They leave the next day departing from Sloo on the 'Sea Queen', then by train from Withinghoe Station to Norrington.

Tess, Joan, Monica and Dagmar go with them to be introduced to 'the Nautical Cabin of S.R.S. Reliance', the Sea Ranger Meeting, and to attend parades and the rest of the day is spent there.

Dagmar is able to go as she is given a day off from the Post Office and all four of them enjoy the day and the welcome given to the Sea Rangers by their families.

After a ceremony a telegram arrives from Miss Grimthorpe, inviting the Sea Rangers to Sloo Manor the day before Christmas Eve. Sir George Heaney is arranging transport and covering expenses. The Roman Road has been discovered and the Sea Rangers are wanted for the ceremony of 'Watch of the Wardstaff'.

Tess, Monica, Joan and Dagmar return home with Tom Hathaway, taking the Sea Rangers acceptance of the invitation with them.

They are able to attend three meetings before going back to their school, Millverne, for the Christmas term. They also visit Sir George, who tells them how he was following the line of stones when he had become caught in the mud. He is most grateful to Sam and the Sea Rangers for saving his life and tells them about the information in the lead box, dating from the 1600s. It is evident from the papers recovered that the old wharf was in use then, and the ancient road known but not useable. While the three are back at school Dagmar is able to attend Sea Ranger meetings regularly and she also learns a lot from Sam Borrowdene.

On the day before Christmas Eve the Sea Rangers arrive by coach and the girls at Sloo Manor have decorated the house, where they have a merry meal.

Afterwards they attend the ceremony of the 'Watch of the Wardstaff', taking part by one girl and a local boy being dropped at various points around the locality. The actual Wardstaff is carried round from one pair to another until it arrives back to the vicar, who then awards it to Sam Borrowdene.

Joan is asked to carry it to him on his houseboat and he lashes it to his mast.

They all return to the Manor, where the Sea Rangers obey their skipper's orders in a ceremony when the four girls, Tess, Joan, Monica and Dagmar, make their promises as Sea Rangers:

When the whole ceremony was over Skipper dismissed the parade. The Sea Rangers saluted and broke off and then there was a rush to the four newly enrolled members, and what a reception they had!

Fact or Fiction ?

The fact that the Foreword is written by the Essex County Sea Ranger Coxswain must mean that she has had the chance to read the book in the nineteen forties. She does say that although not many Sea Ranger Crews will achieve such an adventurous career, they could all aim at being able to deal with the same sort of emergencies.

I am sure that anyone involved in sailing a boat with several other people, then as now, would appreciate the real need for someone to be in charge and give the orders and for the others to obey them. This is a safety consideration and also takes into account the experience and knowledge of the person involved.

This book, written after the Second World War, would be published when memories were very fresh of the stalwart work of Sea Rangers in the War Effort, when their knowledge was of very real value in many life and death situations.

Obedience would have been needed then too.

Guides have always accepted obedience as part of belonging to an organization run in an ordered way. A Guide Captain or Lieutenant, at the time this book was written, would give orders and expect them to be obeyed, as would a Patrol or Company Leader. This does not mean a slavish obedience, but obedience in the understanding of the reasons for an order. Guides in camp during the War would observe regulations under which they could continue to camp; camps would need to be held near home and tents might need to be camouflaged, for very good reasons.

Captain would give out the daily orders, which jobs would be done by which Patrol and there would be no question of not doing these jobs, which would help the smooth running of the camp (and leave time for hikes and swimming and camp-fire!). These jobs would mainly be done cheerfully and there are logbooks and photos to prove it. Not every job would of course be attractive and so better shared on a rota basis, emptying chemical toilets or burning rubbish was no more attractive then than now! Actually the use of trenches then was more likely!

In any community there must be rules for it to run effectively and I am sure that girls of the nineteen forties were well aware of this, coming from schools, where rules certainly applied and breaking them could mean detentions, lines or even the cane. Guiding, as a voluntary activity, has never needed to operate in this way, but I have no doubts that the girls of then were used to obeying and not questioning the instructions given by an adult. Remember that at this date the school leaving age was still fourteen and many girls began work at that early age and would certainly obey an employer. Guiding for them was a fun activity with opportunities for adventure and they would co-operate fully in all its activities, at work or play.

Chapter 11

The Eighth Guide Law
'A Guide smiles and sings under all difficulties'

The Sunshine Shop - by Mrs A.C.Osborn Hann

One of the more prolific writers of Guide fiction stories was Mrs A.C.Osborn Hann. She was born Dorothy Owen in London in 1893, marrying in 1911 the Rev. Archie Cecil Osborn Hann. He was a curate, then a Forces Chaplain and then in 1919 a vicar in a South London slum parish. He had various moves until his retirement in 1939 and death in 1943. His wife later re-married and lived on until 1963.

She had her own Guide Company in South London and, as the vicar's wife, would have been ideally placed to run this, probably attached to her husband's church, as was quite usual then.

In her book 'The Sunshine Shop', first published in 1927,

Mrs Osborn Hann in Guider's Uniform. Note the gauntlets!

which I have in re-print from 1955 by S.W.Partridge & Company, she uses a theme common to a number of Guide stories of the efforts made by a Guide Company or Patrol to continue after their Captain has left.

In this book the main story relates to the Shamrock Patrol of 32nd Southwark Guides introduced at first as Sheila Toop, Patrol Leader, Freda

Mills (Pixie), Lucy (Lugubrious Lucy) according to Sheila, Bertha Browning (Bert), Aggie, and Winnie.

As Guide meetings re-start after a holiday break Sheila is eager to win the Patrol Shield. She is keen that her Patrol should pull them-selves together and show what they are made of! Sheila, beloved by her Patrol, is a working girl:

'Sheila's home was very far from being a happy one, yet she and her mother met all their misfortunes with a smile, and laughed where other people would have cried. Timothy Toop, Sheila's father, had been killed when she was a baby, and Mrs Toop had opened the little fish-shop in East Street, and there she and her daughter stood from morning till night weighing out haddocks, kippers and bloaters. Not a very exciting sort of job, some might think, yet Sheila and her mother had a cheery word for everyone, and never grumbled at the long hours they had to stand there.

Someone had once called the little place the "Sunshine Shop," and the name had stuck ever since.

"Mother would have made a splendid Guide!" Sheila used to say proudly. "She'd never heard of the eighth Guide Law till I joined. Yet she "smiles and sings" all the time, and the more things go wrong, the more she plays up. She'd have been a first-rate Leader."

And Sheila would look admiringly at her bright capable little mother.

"Well. Wot's the good of grizzling?" Mrs. Toop would say. "There's enough sadness in the world without our adding to it! 'Pucker up and whistle' – that's my motto – and a very good one it is!"

Having established early in the story that this is a London Company of working class girls, the reader is introduced to Norah (Norah the Adorer), who works in a factory, where she works with gold paint, which gives her boils.

The first Guide Meeting finds their Captain, Miss Carstairs, not in her usual spirits and in the middle of the evening she announces that the Vicar, Mr Marchant, will be calling to tell them something. This turns out to be the unwelcome news that Miss Carstairs has to go away to Somerset to care for her elderly parents who have been ill. Lieutenant too is leaving as she has a post in another school:

> "Now, Guides," and Mr Marchant's kind brown eyes smiled at the disconcerted girls. " This is a chance to show what stuff you're made of. It's a knockout blow, isn't it, but you aren't going to be knocked out! It's up too to you to put your heads together and see how you're going to carry on. I can't promise you a new Captain until some time after Christmas. The Commissioner hasn't even a spare Lieutenant to send us. But I know you have four splendid Leaders, and I believe you'll be able to carry on for these three or four months. Now, Guides, cheer up! Remember the eighth Guide Law and try to keep smiling."

Five weeks later the Captain, Miss Carstairs, and the Lieutenant, Miss Gorey, depart after the last Parade night, at which they are given leaving gifts of framed photos of the Guide Company:

> Try as they could, it was very hard to be cheerful, and as one of the Leaders put it, "there were times when the eighth Guide Law seemed a practical impossibility!"

Even the offer of a camp the next summer in Somerset hardly cheers them up, but Miss Carstairs urges the Guides to stick together and give the Patrol Leaders the same loyalty as they have given to her. The Guides sing, "For she's a jolly good fellow" and "Auld Lang Syne" (which probably cheers them up and saddens them again!)

On the next Parade night, after the Leaders have held a Court of Honour and made plans, Sheila tells the Guides that the Leaders will take it in turns to be Captain at each meeting and starts off herself with Company Drill. A surprise supper of sandwiches and lemonade adds to the success of the evening.

Norah goes to Somerset, at Miss Carstairs' invitation, to work as a maid for Miss Carstairs' mother. It will be a chance for her to become healthier and her mother (with six younger children) is happy for her to go. The Shamrock Patrol helps her to prepare by making clothes for her to take and giving her gifts. She settles down there happily, although at first she finds the countryside a strange environment.

The Shamrock Patrol flourishes and produces its own Patrol Magazine.

Mrs Toop, Sheila's mother, gives a temporary home to an elderly homeless couple, Mr and Mrs. Baylis and their dog Nell, after inviting them in and giving them tea:

> Mrs Baylis was past hearing the conversation. Worn out by her long tramp, she had succumbed to the comfort of the easy chair and the warm room, and had fallen asleep.
>
> Mrs Toop and Sheila felt the tears come into their eyes at the sight of that wan, haggard face, so pitifully lined.
>
> Just supposing that they were ever to be "down and out" like that! Into Mrs Toop's mind flashed the old text - "Inasmuch as ye do it unto one of these, my little ones, ye do it unto Me." And into Sheila's head came the words: " A Guide is a friend to all."

Obligingly Miss Carstairs offers the couple employment with her parents in Somerset as gardener and cook.

Norah comes home for a two weeks' visit and her Patrol and mother are glad to see she is well and happy.

In the summer the Guides go to camp in Somerset by train with their new Captain, Miss Thompson, discovering a boy stowaway under their seats. They decide to tell the stationmaster but the boy runs away.

Lucy is taken ill and has to go back home by car with Miss Thompson, leaving them with their old Captain, Miss Carstairs. The Guides enjoy their camp, collecting wood for the fires, making gadgets and doing all the inevitable jobs pleasant and unpleasant:

" GOODNESS ! " CRIED PIXIE, " THERE'S SOMEONE UNDERNEATH ! "

page 63

123

The Q.M. was much amused at the efforts of the Heather Patrol, who were responsible for the incinerator and pig-bucket. They had made a notice board, which they stuck into the ground near the refuse pit, and printed on it in huge letters:

YOU *put the Rubbish here. WE Incin!*

"You see, Cap," explained Emma, their Leader, "The Guides would keep dumping all the rubbish in the incinerator when at least half of it could have gone in the pig-bucket. Now there'll be no mistake." And she surveyed her handwork proudly.

"I like inthinning," put in a small Guide with a lisp. "It's awful fun."

They have fun on hikes and walks, do country dancing and have campfires. They learn tracking and stalking and even rescue a lost Wolf Cub! They survive a heavy storm (and remember to loosen the guy-lines except for one Patrol whose tent falls in on them!). They visit Cheddar Caves and, when the lights go out unexpectedly, leave Aggie and Winnie behind and have to go back for them.

Camping in bell tents, complete with centre poles.

They have a Visitors' Day attended by the Vicar of the parish, Mr. and Mrs. Carstairs, the Baylises and village girls who hope one day to be Guides. The Camp Adviser also visits.

Their last day is on a lovely Sunday, when the Guides go to the 8 a.m. church service, spend a day in the woods and go to Evensong at 6.30.

They travel back home after striking their tents and tidying the site. Leaving behind the blue sky, green fields, country lanes and glorious sunshine they return to London:

'A smoky sky, dirty streets, squalid dwellings, pouring rain, that was what awaited them in London.

But nothing could damp the ardour of their spirits. They sang at the top of their voices all the way home, remembering the presents they had bought for every-body, and all the stories they had to tell of Camp.

Dingy, dirty London, but – 'Home!'

These Guides truly knew how to 'smile and sing' under difficulties!

As the following comes from the same book 'The Sunshine Shop' I am going to quote now the full text of a Campfire Ceremony that interprets all the Guide Laws.

At the last campfire of the week several of the Guides take part in a special Campfire Ceremony, one used by them before:

"Draw your ground-sheets in a bit," said Miss Carstairs, "so we get into a smaller circle. There, that's right."

From the darkness behind them came the sound of voices singing softly, "All Through the Night." At the head of the procession walked Sheila, bearing a lighted taper. Still singing, they entered the circle opposite the fire and halted.

"Who are ye," inquired the Captain, "Who comes out of the darkness bearing a shining light?"

And Sheila replied:

"We are the Guide Law. We bring the spirit that dwells in the midst of the Guide Camp; we bear the Light that shines before every Guide to show her the way."

"Lead on, Guide Law," said the Captain, "and give us of thy light."

As each Guide, representing one of the Laws, came up to Sheila with her unlighted taper, and, kneeling, kindled it from hers, the circle of listening girls watched intently.

It was an impressive scene. Darkness all around, star-shine above, silence enfolding the Camp, and within the circle, Sheila, with her lighted taper and pale, earnest face, intensely alive to the solemnity of the moment.

She beckoned to Joan who represented the first Guide Law. The Leader of the Fuchsias came slowly forward, knelt before Sheila, and lighted her taper. Then, holding it aloft, she said distinctly:

"*I am HONOUR, and I shine that a Guide may be trusted in all things, both great and small.*"

With one accord the other Guides raised their tapers and said together:

"*A Guide's Honour is to be trusted.*"

Next came Emma, knelt, lighted her taper from Sheila's, and repeated:

"*I am LOYALTY, and I shine that a Guide may always be found faithful.*"

And together the Guides chanted:

"*A Guide is loyal.*"

Rosie, her round laughing face unusually serious, followed.

"*I am USEFULNESS, and I shine that Guides may at all times learn the joy of Service.*"

As they raised their tapers, the Guides chimed in:

"*A Guide's duty is to be useful and help others.*"

Then Bertha approached, and, kneeling like the rest, said:

"*I am FRIENDLINESS, and I shine that Guides of all nations may know the true Bond of Fellowship.*"

And the others responded:

"*A Guide is a Friend to all and a sister to every other Guide.*"

Lily came next to kneel before Sheila.

"*I am COURTESY,*" she said, "*and I shine that the true Courtesy, born of love and reverence, may grow up within the hearts of the Guides.*"

"*A Guide is courteous,*" said the rest in chorus.

Sylvia, Emma's Second, next approached:

"*I am KINDNESS,*" she said, "*and I shine that the Guides may learn the true love of all God's creatures,*"

"*A Guide is a Friend to Animals,*" chanted the Guides with upraised arms.

Little Dena came next, and said in a shy, shaking voice: *"I am OBEDIENCE, and I shine that Self-control may be the great inward strength of all the Guides."*

And the others replied:

"A Guide obeys orders."

As Dena rose from her knees, Norah came forward to take her place. As she lighted her taper, she said:

"I am CHEERFULNESS, and I shine that every Guide may take the light of Joy wheresoever she goes."

And the Guides chimed in:

"A Guide smiles and sings under all difficulties."

Singing around the Camp Fire. Note the smart best uniform!

Then Winnie came proudly forward, very self-assured and fluent:

"I am Thrift," she said, *"and I shine that a Guide may never waste, but that she may use all she has in the service of others."*

Last came Lydia, the Daffodil second, and spoke her lines distinctly:

"I am PURITY, and I shine that a Guide may be as Light itself, clean, pure, and strong, worthy of her Womanhood."

Then all together, with lighted tapers, their right arms raised, the Guides chanted solemnly:

"A Guide is pure in thought, in word, and in deed."

"Well met, Guide Law," said the Captain. *"You have shown us that without you there is no true Guiding. Stay with us."*

And Sheila, her brown eyes shining, replied:

"We are always here. Our light glows in the heart of every campfire and shines in the eyes of every true Guide."

Then the procession filed slowly by and passed into the darkness, singing softly the strains of *"All Through the Night."* Softer and softer it came, till at last it died away altogether.

127

Fact or Fiction ?

How realistic are the descriptions of this London Guide Company? Very realistic I would think, after all Mrs Osborn Hann was the vicar's wife in a slum parish and drew from her own experiences with her own Guide companies.

In the year this book was written, 1927, girls left school generally at 14, unless in private education or having won a scholarship and the Patrol Leaders in a Guide Company could well be around 15 or 16 years old. This is unlike today when the age group for Guides is 10 to 14 years.

Sheila, the Patrol Leader of the Shamrocks, is a working girl, working full time in a Fish Shop. Patrol Leaders who worked like this were adults and a big help in running a Guide Company.

Other features in the book are also true to life for those days   it would not be uncommon for a family like the Carstairs to have a maid, a cook and a gardener/handyman. My mother's own Guide Captain lived with her sister and parents in a large hillside house with a 'tin hut' where the Guides met. This particular Guide Captain married an Irishman who inherited a baronetcy and she continued her Guiding in Ireland.

Florrie Ford was a London Guide in a very similar Company. Born in 1909, her memories in her eighties were as clear as if it all took place yesterday.

Through all her long life she had made the best of things and truly smiled and sang under all difficulties!

She remembered joining 7th Wandsworth (Earlsfield) Guides at the age of 11 and continuing until she went into service at the age of 14. She left school on her 14th birthday - 21st December 1923 - and started work in January 1924.

The Guide Company was attached to St John the Divine Church, but held meetings in a tin hut at Bendon Valley. There is a road called Bendon Valley in Wandsworth (Earlsfield) today, barely a quarter of a mile from St. John's Drive.

They had about 18 girls, in four Patrols with two officials, a Captain and a Lieutenant, who came to meetings from Streatham by tram. She was soon asked to be Patrol Leader of the Lily of the Valley Patrol and remembered the knotting - the reef knots, sheet bend and bowline - and the badges earned

- Child Nurse and Laundress, but failing her Cook's Badge! They did Drill and went to Church Parade and paid subs of one old penny a week!

Florrie Ford.
Leader of the Lily of
the Valley Patrol.

Highlights were the three camps she went to, once going by lorry to a big house at Chessington (where the zoo is now). They only had one tent so slept in the cowsheds- the cows outside in the summer fortunately! They stuffed palliasses with straw to sleep on and took it in turns to fetch wood and cook. A Russian Princess lived nearby and gave them cheese and biscuits to share at campfire; this was a real treat. I have been unable so far to check where the Princess lived, but understand that some large houses in the area may have been demolished in the 1930s and since.

The second camp was at Mickleham in Surrey and they had borrowed tents so this was better. Her parents came to visit her this time and the Guides went to the local church on Sunday. The third camp was at Oxshot in Kent and it poured with rain, so they came home after a few days. They went on the local greengrocer's lorry and it took them under the Thames through the Blackwall Tunnel.

One year the Patrol Leaders were given a shilling each to double and she did knitting, the garments being sold at a fete.

They did bandaging and Morse code and put on a concert.

She remembered going to a Rally at Streatham, taking their Union Jack and being inspected by a Commissioner with other local Companies.

She had enjoyed the campfire and they had sung 'Be Prepared shall be your Watchword - let us sing it every day!'

After she went to work in service she went to Guide meetings sometimes when she had her time off. Her first job was as a general maid at a college, when she slept in an attic up three flights of stairs. To better her-self after a year she went to a house near Wimbledon Common as under-housemaid, again sleeping in the attic, but she learned to do housework and to wait at table. Her last job before she married was in the house of a Lord in Eton Place.

Her life story would fill a book! She married during the War as her husband was in a reserved occupation on the land, and like many Londoners they lived through the Blitz. They were also bombed out and lost a lot of her china and belongings. She had to register for War Work and chose to work in a canteen, which suited her cheerful attitude.

After the War they moved around with her husband's job and so they finally moved to Malvern, which was where we met, living next door for a while and then in the same village. She and my mother were the best of friends and shared an interest in Guiding. She was always cheerful and even the illnesses of old age never dulled that Guide Spirit.

Chapter 12

The Ninth Guide Law
'A Guide is Thrifty'

Pippa in Switzerland - by E.E.Ohlsen

This is the second of four books telling the story of Pippa and was published in 1938 by Nelson. The stories are told in the first person and are amusing, with a heroine who is always ready to help and proud of being a Guide. Like all well meaning folk she can also be exasperating and a trial to her close relatives!

My copy is undated and undedicated, but in pristine condition with a good dust jacket.

The connection with the Guide Law in this case is not a serious one but humorous.

Pippa returns to her home in Regent's Park after her first term at

Dustwrapper of this book shows Pippa in a short-sleeved uniform.

Boarding School in Brighton, pleased to be back home. She finds out that her family are going on holiday to Switzerland, but that she is to stay in Lowestoft with her Aunt Florence. Her sister, Nita, has been unwell since she stayed with Aunty Mary in Bristol in May, and the complete change and mountain air may improve her health. Another sister, Muriel, who is engaged to the painter Charles Reeves, is to go away to France with his people.

A family friend called Maggie Crawley, who is also to be in the Swiss party, comes to tea and Pippa introduces Switzerland into the conversation after she has eaten three helpings of curry:

> Maggie screwed up her mouth into a round button, and looked at Mother. "Isn't she going?" she inquired.
>
> "Well, no. You see, Aunt Florence has asked her to spend her holidays at Lowestoft - which is a very nice, healthy, bracing place"
>
> "Oh," said Maggie, making a face, "I think she'd better come with us, don't you know. A Swiss tour is so frightfully educational, it would be a pity for her to miss it at her age."
>
> "But it's so expensive," argued Mother. "And Pippa is so tiresome on a journey."

Pippa protests that she is not and that she is a Girl Guide. She does agree however to leave her uniform at home, and will only carry her stout Guide heart!

She decides to take an alpenstock and, without her father's knowledge, takes one of his walking sticks.

When her father comes home he says he cannot go to Switzerland, but the others can go on ahead. His wife decides to stay behind to travel with him to meet them later.

Pippa later on cuts notches on the walking stick with her Guide knife and hammers nails in the end. She also hammers nails into the soles of her walking shoes, which makes them uncomfortable. I doubt that this is in any way thrifty, although I'm sure Pippa could justify this, as she has clearly saved her parents the cost of an alpenstock or nailed boots! However the fact that she has ruined a good walking stick and a pair of shoes contradicts this, as does the fact that she causes damage in the house walking round to try them out:

> "They were not very comfortable to wear when I had finished, it is true. But then one cannot expect the drawing-room carpet, or even the linoleum in the hall to present the same surface as an iceberg. I practised in them for an hour before wrapping them up carefully in a Morning Post and stowing them away in my case."

Thinking about food for the journey, she goes to see Cook in the kitchen, hoping to make up a hamper. However Cook is in a bad mood and refuses to give her a cooked chicken she knows is in the pantry, telling her not to go in the pantry. Pippa is not deterred, slipping back to take the chicken and wrapping it in her hanky!

"And I count it as one of my good Guide deeds."

The Swiss party leaves from Victoria Station, Maggie so excited that she keeps breaking into a dance. Pippa asks her father for some Swiss currency and he gives her some small change. They see a clergyman also catching the train with a party of ladies and Maggie offers to help him as he tries to round them up. He laughs when Maggie asks if they are affiliated to the Mother's Union.

They have to sit in a carriage with other people:

"I grew very hot. It was not only the stuffiness of the crowded carriage, but also the weight and thickness of the clothes I was wearing. No one had guessed, up to the present, that my travelling coat and skirt were worn over the good Guide uniform, I was the only sufferer, and it certainly was uncomfortable all bundled up so that I could hardly breathe.

I was carrying the alpenstock, which I had covered with brown paper and lashed to three old umbrellas I had found that did not belong to anyone. I had tied the little brown chicken round my waist between my two skirts, and it dangled against my upper legs very uncomfortably.

On the train journey Pippa shares her grapes with Maggie, who has left hers on the seat and an old gentleman is sitting on them! She also offers her a slice of chicken, which Maggie refuses, although she is curious to know what is in the mound on Pippa's lap. Once on the boat at Newhaven Pippa hides behind a funnel to take off her coat and skirt and ties them on the umbrellas and alpenstock:

"It was certainly much more comfortable without them, and I strode the deck proudly and felt that I was a worthy type of the girlhood of old England. The chicken, tied up in a Morning Post, could now be seen suspended from my belt."

When Pippa has a walk round the deck she sees Maggie with the party of ladies and she has discovered that the clergyman, the Reverend Arnold Percy, is taking them to Switzerland. They mostly come from his parish.

Maggie manages to find tea and brioches to eat on the train when the train has an early morning stop, and when they reach Paris they see a red-haired young man they have spotted before. Maggie mistakes him for the train conductor when he holds open an omnibus door for them and tells them to go to Gare de l'Est, where they will get the dinner they have booked. After eating they cross the busy road to the railway station and find a compartment, which becomes crowded when six of Mr Percy's party also squeeze in. The redheaded young man also tries to come in, but sees Nita, who has her eyes closed, and he quickly leaves. Pippa continues to offer slices of her chicken, but Nita asks where she has got this from, and, seeing it hanging from Pippa's belt in newspaper, she refuses it.

Arriving at Basle, Pippa follows the smell of coffee and is carrying most of the bags. She has an exchange of words with one of the old ladies who wants her to carry her suitcase.

They have coffee and rolls and Pippa eats five, and puts as many as she can in her coat pockets for future use. When Maggie and Nita queue for the Customs check she slips away to explore the platform and see if the mountains are in view. She finds the redheaded young man sitting alone smoking and, chatting to him, discovers he is Nita's boyfriend. The two had met at Bristol and were to be engaged, but had quarrelled. Pippa thinks that this accounts for Nita's behaviour all summer and he tells her that he is called Maurice Lester and is an artist. They talk and Pippa offers to help him and, as he looks hungry, offers him some of the rolls from her pocket and the parcel containing the little brown chicken:

> "I slithered away, but just as I was crawling under the barrier I happened to look in his direction, and it seemed to me that he was depositing with great care and secrecy the rolls and the chicken at

the back of a truck, where they wouldn't be noticed. I daresay my eyes deceived me, for, of course, he wouldn't do such a thing. A meal like that wouldn't be likely to come his way every day."

When Pippa joins the others there is a delay while Maggie finds her keys and they retrieve Pippa's luggage, then they board the train. Nita seems very sad and the others become hungry, Pippa eats her rolls and Maggie some soft biscuits.

Pippa tries to cheer Nita up:

"Nita," I said, "you shall have some nourishment as soon as I can get it for you. I regret very much that the chicken I brought for you is now past recall."

"What chicken?" asked Nita listlessly.

"One that our cook had cooked and left on the pantry shelf. I lifted it with my own hands and tied it up. I carried it dangling round my waist as far as Basle, and there, instead of giving it to you and Maggie, I rashly and thoughtlessly bestowed it on one who, I greatly fear, did not appreciate it. I acted on impulse."

"I don't know what you're talking about," said Nita, "and I'm sure I don't want to. If you really had a chicken in the disgusting newspaper parcel, I can but be thankful that you have got rid of it."

It's no good looking for gratitude in this world, as we Guides know only too well, but I was a little downcast when I rejoined Maggie at the window.

They arrive at Interlaken settling into the hotel where Mr Percy and his group of ladies are also staying and Pippa continues to eat as much as she can. She also asks Nita if she likes the name of Maurice and sees her start violently and blush. From this point in the story the only real thriftiness is that practised by Pippa, which might also be called greed, when she enjoys lots of meals and snacks. She also squirrels away food in her pockets at any opportunity for later consumption!

They explore the town, visiting the church on Sunday and also see some lace makers. Pippa has arranged to meet Maurice Lester in the hotel lounge and they go outside to sit on a restaurant balcony, where she asks if he enjoyed the chicken. He is rather puzzled but polite and buys her an ice cream.

They talk about Nita and what went wrong with their friendship. This turns out to be that they had quarrelled over his wanting to paint, but he now knows he will have to give this up for a regular job. They arrange for Pippa to take the others up the Harder Mountain, so that Nita can bump into Maurice, who plans to go up to do some sketching.

Maggie is becoming friendly with the clergyman's party, and the next day one of the lady members asks if she can join Maggie, Nita and Pippa as she doesn't want to go to Grindelwald with the rest. The lady, Mrs Wilson Carrington, takes a liking to Pippa and when Pippa helps her to choose gifts for her family, gives them all to her. Mrs Carrington has left her husband and children at home and seems sad and Pippa decides to send her husband a telegram to say his wife needs him. She finds out the name of his daughter and also says to bring her. She finds the address out from the hotel visitor's book and feels very pleased with herself!

> "It made a frightful inroad on my resources to pay for this, and I had very little money left, but I felt I was doing a good deed and the whole Guide movement was glorified by it."

In the afternoon they go on a steamer on Lake Brienz and, in the town of Brienz, buy carved animals, made of wood, have tea at a hotel then travel back to Interlaken. At dinner Mrs Carrington receives a telegram and later tells them the good news that her husband is joining her.

On the next day Pippa is up early to buy tickets for the Harderbahn (funicular) and is at the office before it is open, but the official gives in and serves her. As the others are still in bed she borrows Maggie's camera and takes pictures around the hotel and is invited to the kitchen for a cup of coffee.

The cook gives her frothy coffee and brioches and she does not eat too many "as it would never do to have no appetite for breakfast." She does manage a little breakfast with Maggie and Nita and tells them that she has bought the tickets for the funicular up the Harder Mountain.

Nita is not keen to go and complains a lot, but they set off and arrive at a plateau where they see golden eagles soaring in the sky above. Pippa is hungry again and eats sugary buns and chocolate biscuits.

When they go for a walk finally Pippa spots Maurice working at a picture and pretends to be falling, which alarms Maggie and Nita who rush to help her. Maurice springs towards Nita, as she is in danger, and they end up in each other's arms. Maggie is alarmed at this but Pippa explains that they are in love and have had a quarrel, then a happy Nita and Maurice join them and this calls for more food for Pippa!

Pippa's scheming has succeeded brilliantly, as has her meddling in the Carrington's affairs since, back at the hotel, Mrs Carrington is with her husband and daughter, Elizabeth, and very happy.

Pippa and Elizabeth make friends and, planning to go to Grindelwald the next day and to see the glacier, she persuades Elizabeth to make an alpenstock from her father's umbrella. Elizabeth is not persuaded to hammer nails into her shoes!

The next day the whole group go to Grindelwald and Pippa has managed to obtain a hamper full of food. After a meal with Maggie, Nita and Maurice, the girls slip off, giving an excuse and make for the glacier taking the hamper.

They are caught in a storm and the mist comes down and Pippa blows her Guide whistle for help, a reply coming from a boy called James looking for his friend nicknamed Spider. They are camping out in a hut and Spider has gone to find food. James takes the girls to the hut when he sees they have food and starts to eat it, then Spider arrives, having dropped his hamper down a crevasse.

Spider has seen people looking for the girls and, when the sun comes out and the mist clears, the four of them begin to walk back. They are met by Maggie and Nita, who are very relieved, and then by Maurice and two mountain guides. They return to the station and the boys slip away While waiting for the train to Interlaken they go into a restaurant where Pippa excels herself by ordering a sand cake:

> "Not in slices, but in its entirety. Its shape is that of a fat yellow ring,
> it has a hole in the middle, and it is quite dry, like white sand, and

very sweet. Maggie and Nita did not care for it, but Elizabeth and I did ample justice to it, and I packed up all that was left in my Guide's wallet. You never know when a thing will come in handy."

Maurice joins them and eats ham sandwiches and tells them that, when the girls were thought lost, Elizabeth's parents had been told and had planned to come to Grindelwald to search for them. They have been told to wait for further news as everything possible is being done. Now they have been told they would all be back by the last train:

"What a very nice-looking sandwich you've got there, Maurice," I interposed. "I like them made of scooped-out rolls and filled with ham. Are you going to eat it or not?"

"I am not," replied Maurice. "I am one of those who know when they have had enough."

"Then would you just pass it to me?" I asked. "For waste is foreign to my nature, and though I don't propose to eat it on the spot, it will probably come in useful when I am in bed."

Maurice passed the delicacy, but he seemed astonished. "Do you eat sandwiches in bed?" he asked.

"Of course, when I'm lucky enough to get them, but it's generally sweets. There's a shop at Brighton where they sell hardbake."

"Is there?" said Maurice, shuddering. "I hope I shall never go near it."

"Well, when you're at school you have to do the best you can," I said. "Don't you like hardbake, Maurice?"

"I don't know what it is, but I'm quite sure I shouldn't like it," he answered, and watched me with curiosity as I put the sandwich in my wallet with the sand cake.

They return to a warm welcome at Interlaken and the next day the two girls go out shopping and after lunch follow Mr Percy's party to the landing stage for the steamer, near the railway at Interlaken. They have a few small adventures on the boat across Lake Thun.

On the Saturday they travel to Lucerne to meet Pippa and Nita's parents and Maurice is introduced to them. The boys, James and Spider, also arrive and Pippa's father invites them to a picnic on the lake. Meanwhile the two girls and boys go out to explore and to look at the shops.

The picnic the next day goes well and there is plenty to eat, and so the holiday ends. Pippa says that:

> "I should dread going back to England and leaving all this, if I didn't know that I should enjoy everything that happens to me and have a good time wherever I happen to be."

Fact or Fiction ?

The adventures of Pippa are most definitely fictional, although her overwhelming interest in food and the next meal is very familiar. It is not also unknown for food to be tucked away for later, although stuffed in a pocket or hanging in a parcel from your belt for several days is not recommended!

Also we all know that, while necessity is the mother of invention, the 'borrowing' of a walking stick to make an alpenstock and putting nails in your shoes is not really the thing.

However the idea of being thrifty would not be new to a girl of the 1930s or indeed her parents as thrift was a necessity for most families and 'waste not, want not' well known.

Both Lord and Lady Baden-Powell commenting on the Law "A Guide is Thrifty" pointed out in their writings a Guide must make the most of her possessions, never wasting anything, and learn to manage her money and to save for a rainy day. This will also mean she can help others when the need arises. Lady Baden-Powell stresses that this is a patriotic thing too and also by helping conserve national resources the real value of things is realised. This includes our time, given to us to use and not waste.

In a short story by May Marshall, published by 'The Girl's Own Paper' in a book of Twenty-Six Girl Guide Stories, we can see that Guides have understood at least the basics of being thrifty. In the story 'The Letters that Crossed' Molly writes from Somerset to her school chum, Jeanne, telling her about Guides:

"When you read the laws you may be scared when you get to number nine - 'A Guide is thrifty.' Of course that means you won't be able to 'borrow' any more from your hapless form mates in order to buy your everlasting bijouterie, hair slides and what not. But think how good for you that will be, and what a pleasant change when the Head doles out pocket-money on Saturday if you haven't to pass it all on to your various creditors. No, mon enfant, a Guide never behaves that way; she not only makes her pocket-money last the whole week, but she manages to spend some of it on others - and even to SAVE. I hope this doesn't sound too frightening, but I thought I ought to warn you, as I'm sure that is the Guide Law you will find hardest to keep."

There were also a number of Guide Badges in which thrift was a part. There was 'Cobbler', one clause relating to soling and heeling a pair of boots or shoes and being able to repair them, 'Domestic Service' and 'Handywoman.'

Part of 'Homemaker' required that the Guide could mend household linen, cloths, curtains etc. Among the badges involving thrift were also 'Laundress' and 'Needlewoman' which included the sewing of a patch in cotton or other material, darning a sock or stocking and making an item of clothing. I recall the hours I spent over a patch or a darn before I felt it good enough for the tester!

'Thrift' Badge itself was an annual badge and to keep it you needed to add at least 2/6d a year to your savings. The badge required regular saving out of earnings or pocket money of at least 15/6d and a letter detailing work done for the badge. You also had to take to the test something made out of odd pieces of material and then satisfy the tester that you did understand the real meaning of thrift. Amongst the ideas suggested was using up newspapers - one suggestion was to put them inside a thin coat for insulation!

The Guide Association in the Second World War took part in much salvage of used materials to help the War Effort - jam jars, newspapers, clothes and also fruit picking. Growing up after the War many of the economies were still practised and I was familiar with something made from parachute silk - it made a lovely dressing up outfit. Also rugs were still made out of rags and feather-beds received new covers - ticks - and I can still see my mother and a neighbour outside stuffing the feathers in! Sheets were machined sides to middle and very uncomfortable it was too if you were on the join! Sour milk was used for pancakes, although we drew the line at that! They still tasted disgusting. This was before the fridge became a necessity in every home and milk was kept on the cold slab in the larder and scalded in summer to keep it useable, meat in a meat-safe and butter in a butter-cooler.

Today we are constantly reminded that resources are finite and we need to re-use and re-cycle. To the Guide of the 1930s this was a way of life, not to save the planet, but needed in an age of homes with one income and that not very high in many cases.

Girls were brought up to observe these ways of saving and as many left school at fourteen they would still be of Guide age then, with the age limits eleven to sixteen. After this they would be a Senior Guide or a Ranger and the badge syllabus would be much the same   the badges would have red on them instead of the early olive green then dark green.

Chapter 13

The Tenth Guide Law
'A Guide Keeps Herself Pure in
Thought, Word and Deed'

Mary Court's Company - by Elizabeth Walmsley

In 'Girl Guiding', the official Handbook by Lord Baden-Powell, first issued in 1918, this Guide Law is explained quite simply:

> She (a Guide) should train herself to look for what is beautiful in everything, so that she may become strong enough in her mind to avoid listening to, or taking part in anything that is ugly and unclean.

Elizabeth Walmsley's book was written in 1925 and published by The Pilgrim Press. My copy has blue linen boards with gold patterns on the front and the handwritten dedication is to 'Miss Eva Mumby, a small recognition for her Services in Dry Doddington Church Choir January 1926 - New Year.' The printed dedication is to 'The Commandant, Guiders and Guides of the Group Camp, Wrabness, Essex. The Foreword is by K.Daniels, Essex C.C.A. (County Camp Adviser) and reads:

> 'It is interesting to note, as the Guide Movement grows, and claims year by year a larger share in the youthful life of the nation, and a greater amount of public interest, how the guide motive is creeping into contemporary fiction.
>
> Such a story as Mary Court's Company may well help to illustrate the activities of the movement, because the author has studied guiding at very close quarters - even spending a week in a guide camp.
>
> I think therefore, this story should appeal to guides, both young

and old, being founded - for all that has to do with guiding - on facts. To some it will bring memories of a group camp in Essex this summer; to others, who are not guides, it should awaken the desire to join the great sisterhood, which stands for adventure and service one to another.'
November 1924.

Elizabeth Walmsley wrote her books over a short period on subjects including Guides, and was a Guider in Essex. She and the Essex Camp Adviser would have known each other. This was in the early days of Guiding, the Movement dating from only 1910.

The story is set in a town of factories, Wroxton, and begins with two girls, Janie Thwaite and Violet Marks, leaving school for the day. Janie is urging Violet to steal some sweets from the market, which she thinks is easy and fun. Neither come from families who will freely give money for sweets. Violet is reluctant but loves sweets and wants to be popular with Janie. She watches Janie take some chocolates but, when she tries, she is seen and both girls drawn away by three older girls. They are told that it is wrong, and one of the girls, wearing a Guide Promise Badge, sees the need for these and other children to be organised to do something good - in this case Girl Guides. She says she will come along to their school and talk to their teacher, Miss Dester, but will not 'tell on them.' She makes them promise not to steal again:

VIOLET DARTED FORWARD, ONLY TO FIND HERSELF . . . CAUGHT.
—*Page* 18.

"On your honour," the clear urgent voice admonished her; 'you know what 'honour' means, don't you, Janie?"

Janie did apparently, for she nodded her head, but the idea seemed too hazy to explain in more explicit terms. The big girl laughed and forbore to press the point.

"That's the place where we begin," she declared, turning to the others; "that's the foundation of the whole thing."

She stood up straight, as though it was finished, and smiled at the children.

"Janie Thwaite" she said, noting the name, "and Violet Marks. I shan't forget, and don't you forget me; I am Doctor Court's sister, and my name is Mary. We are going to know each other very well quite soon, and be friends." She also tells them that they can look forward to something gorgeous and much better than sweets. The dazzled children decide that they like her and Janie feels ashamed as she would like Mary to trust her.

Once home from school Janie talks to her brother, Bob, who is scathing about both Scouts and Girl Guides. Janie works on some minor sewing to gloves her mother makes up as outwork, working also at Fordman's factory; Mrs Thwaite needs help as her husband is away at sea and there is little money coming into the house. Her older daughter, Hetty, at 16, works in the glove factory, but is vain and spends her money on herself.

Her mother doesn't mind her going to the Pictures, but doesn't like her staying out late and associating with a boy called Phil Ogden who is known to be no good.

She is also concerned that Hetty is so vain, looking at herself in the mirror so much and tries to talk to her, but Hetty, in a temper, breaks her mother's milk jug. Bob stops her from doing anything else and Mrs Thwaite is tired of the quarrels.

Into this pandemonium comes Mary Court, who has come to look for Hetty who lets her in, as she has heard that Mary has been friendly when she called at the factory where Hetty works. Mary wants to tell her about Guiding as she hopes to start a Guide Company there. She has been the Captain of a Guide Company at Beechwood, the famous Girls School she attended her-self, but has now moved to Wroxton to keep house for her young bachelor brother, a doctor.

Miss Dester at Broughton Road Schools, where Janie Thwaite goes to school, and old Doctor Sargent, in partnership with Doctor Court, are both captivated by Mary Court and her enthusiasm:

> To say that there was some excitement at Fordman's, when at last it transpired that Mary Court was going to hold a meeting and tell them all about the Girl Guides, was to put it mildly. The gay little figure had already become a sort of embodied promise to not a few of the girls like Hetty Thwaite, who knew her personally, and had been preaching the gospel of a good time coming for all of them, to each and several of their workmates for the last few weeks.

Some of the older women were disparaging about 'Girl Guides', with objections to 'Girl soldiers' and 'having a good time', but even they praised Mary Court.

Mrs Thwaite is only too pleased that Hetty is interested in Mary Court's ideas and at Broughton Road School both children and teachers are interested. However Mary has a problem as there are plenty of schoolchildren wanting to be Brownies and Guides, and in the factories girls wanting to be Rangers, but she needs Guiders first of all.

She is determined that the teacher, Miss Dester, shall be a 'Brown Owl' and her sister 'Tawny Owl' but needs to look further for help with Guides.

She obtains the use of a big packing room at the factory and the Guide Company from her old school will come along to give a demonstration. They will camp for a week in a field at the bottom of Doctor Sargent's garden. Miss Dester is enthusiastic and agrees to go up to the field where the Guides will camp to help put up some tents. She says:

> "How jolly! I'd like to awfully! Isn't 'campcraft' part of the training?"
>
> "Yes, and a very big part. When we get really started here, and everything is going well, camping will be the grand thing to plan and look forward to. It's going to do these factory girls no end of good."

Mary Court's doctor brother is a Scoutmaster and takes his Scouts to Wroxton Station to welcome the visiting Guide Company. One of his Scout Patrol Leaders has been given a reward of £5 for finding some jewellery, and, while he does not expect reward for being honest, he offers this to Mary Court to start her Guide funds. Mary Court is:

Pretty as a picture in her neat dark coat and skirt, the upturned hat with its smart cockade, workmanlike leather belt and gauntleted brown gloves. A flush of unwonted colour dyed her cheeks, and her eyes sparkled.

Pretty as a picture in her neat dark coat and skirt, the upturned hat with its smart cockade, workman like leather belt and gauntleted brown gloves. Picture from another Guide story of the time.

When the train arrives she is pleased to meet her best friends, Marjorie Foster and Genevieve (commonly called Jenny). Marjorie had been her Guide Lieutenant, and is now Captain of the school company, but asks Mary to take charge of the camp.

Mary is to camp with them and tells her friends of her plans to first form a cadet corps for guiders:

"That's where you come in. I badly want you to help me decide about them. Some are exactly the right sort, and will make splendid officers, but others give me to think furiously. There's one girl in particular - Hetty Thwaite, I can't make up my mind about her; but you'll like Nellie Dester, a little school-teacher here, A1".

The camp is soon set up and the colour ceremony takes place, after which

Mary thanks them for coming to help her in Wroxton. She tells them about the girls in the town and that she needs them to share guiding with the town's girls, who have none of their advantages:

> "You know how, if we can share the joyousness, the purposes, the friendship and the holidays of guiding with these Wroxton factory girls, it will enrich our own lives as well as theirs."

She goes on to talk about the help of a uniform and how guiding makes girls equal and how she has in mind a few of the girls here as representative of a large number in Wroxton:

> "They are young and bright and pretty, and full of that very modern envy of the well-to-do which makes for class spite and bitterness, and leads to all sorts of disasters. They haven't any standards, or any healthy interests. That's where Guiding is to come in.

A very important meeting takes place at Fordman's factory, with the Scouts forming an avenue for the Guide Company to march in. Mr Fordman himself acts as chairman, introducing Commissioner, Lady St. John, who speaks about the Guide Movement and talks about the training it gives:

> "Every girl who aspires to be a guide must make up her own mind to be in earnest, to enjoy the simple things of life, to find pleasure in unselfishness and duty, and to be done once and for all with everything which would not bear the light. A guide must be truthful, and honest, and pure."

Mary Court outlines her plans for Guiding in Wroxton and that she is to enrol a small number of girls, who will receive a short course of training. She will also take names for those wanting to be guides and they will later be put in patrols under the twenty selected for training.

Lady St. John goes on to take the enrolment, welcoming the girls chosen into the great sisterhood:

> It was not a mere collective ceremony; it was an individual thing.

None of them had been quite prepared for the actual shock of this emotion.

Passionate, impulsive natures like Hetty Thwaite experienced it to the utmost. Her whole heart, her whole loyalty flew into the full salute she then gave in return.

After the enrolment the visiting guides give an impressive demonstration of Morse signalling, then dances and some singing.

The Guide Camp goes well and, one afternoon, some of the factory girls are given time off to see a swimming and lifesaving display in the local river. Hetty tries lifesaving and her vivid colouring and happiness attracts the attention of two onlookers. One is Phil Ogden, who tells the other her name and that she is his young lady and works at Fordman's. He also tells the stranger that Hetty is ambitious and the man makes some notes, not giving a reason for his interest.

The Camp goes by all too quickly, with a campfire for visitors and a dramatic incident when a girl stops a runaway horse. There is also a party for schoolchildren and then the visitors return home.

The Wroxton cadets work hard to set up their Headquarters in the Old Railway Club building and Hetty Thwaite helps organise the working parties. They make a good job of it and then Mary Court tells them of their training scheme.

Mrs Thwaite is pleased that she is now receiving more help from Hetty and Janie, who is working for her tenderfoot test. The training goes well, Lady St.John enrols more girls as guides and the new Headquarters is opened. It attracts publicity and there are even pictures in the Daily Mail!

Hetty Thwaite nearly went out of her mind with excitement. There she was, the patrol-leader of the Daffodils, figuring full-length as "A bonny girl guide," with a smile on her face, as Bob said, "like a toothpaste advertisement."

It was quite the most glorious moment of her existence. She lived in the glory of it for days, and realised to the full all the interest it aroused at the factory. Hetty felt herself to be really something at last, and grew - at one bound - more than equal to the first responsibilities that fell upon her as the leader of a little troop of girls, among whom it was quite nice to have her younger sister. Goodness! How Hetty resolved to look well to the ways of her patrol!

P.Ls 1 Seconds 1934.

The Patrol Leaders and Seconds of a Company in 1934

However all this excitement and the good intentions pale into insignificance when she receives a letter from some film producers, who have been given her name, seen her photograph and want her to try out for a film. Hetty is overcome by this and can see her chance of fame, reading that the author - 'is now selecting an actress for the principal role.'

She remembers the words of Mary Court about Guiding:

"You've got to grasp what you're driving at before you begin."
Hetty grasped it, and the vision flared before her! "All these things will I give thee, if thou wilt but fall down - "

She sees visions of wealth and clothes and being envied. All this however was not in Mary Court's thoughts, but Hetty won't think of this.

Hetty becomes totally hysterical and her behaviour terrifies poor Mrs Thwaite. Janie alone has the sense to throw cold water from a jug over her sister, which does calm her down, but Hetty will not listen to her mother's words of caution. She is determined to go to London and be a cinema star. Mrs Thwaite asks her to talk it over with Mary Court, but Hetty has no intention of doing so:

Hetty gave a sharp exclamation of impatience.

'Miss Court's a dear," she said, "But I don't see as I have any call to consult her about this. She wouldn't know anything about it; and, in any case, I shouldn't have any time for guiding any more. That was all right so long as there wasn't any glimmering of a chance to get away from Wroxton and the factory. Everything's altered now."

Hetty will not listen to her mother, who tries to forbid her to go to live in London and goes upstairs to change, running off to the station.

On the way she sees Phil Ogden at work in the stationer's, Singleton's, and borrows £5 from him for her fare, which he takes from the till.

News of Hetty's departure causes consternation at the factory and amongst the Guides. Mary Court, to whom Mrs Thwaite goes for help, takes her to London, where they find Hetty staying in a Girls' Hostel. They leave a message for her to join them at their hotel for dinner, but she is determined to go ahead with her plans, which are to stay in London for two to three weeks, then to Yorkshire to do film scenes and then to Italy. She is to receive a salary and all the clothes she needs and is full of the film world. Mary Court and Mrs Thwaite find her some better rooms but have no alternative but to return home without her.

Hetty gives no thought to her family, rarely writes and offers them no financial help at all. 'She never sent her mother as much as a sixpence.'

She is greatly missed at Guides, where they feel the loss of her enthusiasm, and the Daffodils have to have a new Patrol Leader. Mary Court misses her too and is very anxious as to what action she should take, writing to Lady St.John:

"In all my experience," she said, "I do not think I have ever heard of a girl being asked to resign her Tenderfoot. It would be dreadful to have to take any such extreme steps as this, and within so short a time of starting the guides in Wroxton. Do please let me have the benefit of your help and advice."

However then something else happens, which leaves them no further option but to do this. Philip Ogden is arrested and prosecuted by his employers for a series of petty thefts and, in the magistrate's court, his betting is mentioned and that he has made gifts and loans to girls. Hetty Thwaite's name is mentioned and the case goes to trial.

Hetty writes in response to the letter Mary Court sends, defending herself from being responsible for Phil's doings and saying that it is an oversight that she has not returned the £5 to him before:

> As for the other matter - the guiding - she really had not had time to give it a moment's thought. She was working tremendously hard. Nobody knew what it was to have a big part in a film production. If Miss Court didn't want her name on the roll any longer, she would certainly return the little brooch, only she was sorry to say it had somehow got mislaid. She sent her love to the girls, and would be sure and let them know when the film was finished and 'released.'

Mary Court has never had such an upset before and her brother comforts her distracting her with a letter he has received from her friend 'Gene' (Genevieve) with whom he has become friendly.

Brown Owl, Miss Dester, helps out at the Wroxton Isolation Hospital in an outbreak of Scarlet Fever and tells the children stories. Some of the patients are her Brownies. Guide meetings continue with great enthusiasm from the girls and leaders and letters to parents away from home reflect this.

Hetty Thwaite by now is in Naples, which is both hot and noisy and is finding that her life is not as glamorous as she hopes it will be. She finds herself ill and alone in the bedroom of a big hotel in Naples, not able to make the hotel servant understand that she needs a maid to look after her. She is miserable and homesick and her eyes have given her problems. The strong arc lights in the studios in England and then the strong Italian sun have affected them and then she has had a mosquito bite on her foot just after arriving in Naples. Her foot has swollen up so that she has been unable to put it to the ground.

Other ladies in the cast are at the same hotel and one, in a minor part, has been asked to look after her but has neglected her. A maid has been engaged for her, but she has preferred to look after Hetty's rival, Miss Delia Lovibond, after discovering that Hetty is an ex factory hand. Finally

Delia does report matters to the Chief, Mr Mortimer, and a doctor sees Hetty and makes it clear that her eyesight is threatened and her foot needs skilled attention. The other ladies in the cast have been jealous of Hetty and Delia has hoped that she will break down. The producer has employed an accomplished movie actress as Hetty's understudy and she will step in. She would have been employed in the first place but for the author's insistence on Hetty:

> One of the reasons why Mary Court's runaway had failed to write home or to headquarters, as she should have done in the initial weeks of her great adventure, was because she had so soon found herself an object of ill will and dislike. It disconcerted Hetty long before it sapped her courage.

She has persevered up to the time of leaving England, but now she has had to give in to illness and homesickness.

Doctor Cuomo, after talking to the film chief, tells Mary gently that her film work is over and that she needs to contact her friends at home. He arranges a nurse for her, a nun from the local convent, Sister Elizabeth, who speaks English.

The nun nurses Hetty back to health and Hetty learns to trust her, but Hetty begins to worry about how she will ever be able to go home. She also thinks about her family and friends and Sister Elizabeth brings her a pile of letters from home. Before the nun opens them to read to her at her request, she wants to tell her kind nurse a little about herself. When she says she is so afraid that her captain will be cross with her and mentions Guides, she discovers that there are Guides in Naples. The captain of the guides is Signorina Concetta Rossi, a great friend of the Mother Superior at the convent. All this brightens Hetty up and when the letters are read they are affectionate from her mother and kind from Mary Court. The long letter from her guide captain tells her all the news and says that Hetty must now write to Signorina Rossi and enclose a letter from Lady St. John:

> "She (Signorina Rossi) will be able to find you some suitable travelling companion, I have no doubt, or put you under the auspices of people who will help you and look after you all the way to Dover. Tell

her you are a guide - for your patrol have unanimously petitioned for you to be reinstated, Hetty, and I am forwarding a Tenderfoot for you to wear again under separate cover. Go and see her if you can. If not, I'm sure she will visit you."

The nurse takes the letter to Concetta Rossi, who comes to see Hetty and they are soon friends. She also takes her out for a drive, protecting her eyes, after obtaining permission from the doctor They meet some of the Italian guides and gradually Hetty is restored to health and spirits. However the Signorina can see how homesick Hetty is; in fact every night she sobs for her mother and for Captain Mary. At last she is told that Signorina Rossi has to go to England for a conference and will take Hetty back home with her:

> "I am so happy to think my journey can serve a double purpose like this. Besides, my dear," as the girl overwhelmed her with expressions of excitement and delight, "we're guides, after all. And this is only guiding!"

Signorina Rossi is a poor traveller and Hetty looks after her on the cross-channel steamer, staying with her even though she could eat a huge meal herself.

Arriving at Dover:

> A very washed out little guide captain was supported tottering down the gang-plank at Dover by a very rosy-cheeked guide, whose whole concern at that moment was to help her set her feet firmly on dry land.

Hetty has not thought anyone will be there to meet her, but Mary Court is there to welcome the signorina with the support of her arm, reaching out to Hetty with the other in a gesture of comradeship. They clamber into the train and while the signorina falls asleep, the other two talk:

> "I know you have forgiven me, Captain, darling, but I have so longed to hear you say so."

The two hands that closed upon her own gave Mary Court's a nervous wring of compunction, love, and unfathomable gladness.

The elder girl moved slightly and passed her arm around the other.

"I have nothing to forgive, Hetty, dear. Look up and let me see no shadow on your face."

On the way to London Hetty shows Mary the gifts she received from the Italian guides and those she has bought herself for her family and friends.

At Victoria Station she is to be met by her mother and Signorina Rossi by Lady St.John, but when the train draws in her whole patrol is there, drawn up just behind her mother:

Hetty gave one spring and had her mother in her arms. Then everything broke up in a glorious confusion of welcome back and welcome home.

Fact or Fiction ?

This Guide Law - keeping oneself pure in thought, word and deed, is certainly well illustrated in the book chosen, for Mary Court herself certainly lives according to this. She is pure and wholesome in appearance and in the words she speaks, always encouraging the girls with whom she is involved to live honest and worthy lives. She gently discourages the children from stealing, offering to them and their older sisters a way of life, in which they will find fulfilment and adventure.

From my research I have no doubts that there were many such Mary Courts in the early days of Guiding. With the First World War over many women had lost sweethearts and many knew they would never marry and put all their energy and enthusiasm into other channels. However Mary Court is a young woman, only two or three years out of education in a Girls Private School, where she has been a Guide, then a Guide Captain.

In those early days boarding schools such as St. James's, West Malvern, were amongst the first to encourage Guiding. Their Headmistress, Miss Alice Baird, met Lord Baden-Powell when he visited Malvern for a Scout

Display. She encouraged the girls to become Baden-Powell Girl Guides and they were first registered in March 1911. Miss Baird became a personal friend of Lord and Lady Baden-Powell and County then Assistant County Commissioner for Worcestershire. Guiding flourished with virtually the whole school involved.

Miss Alice Baird began Cadets for the older girls, training them to be Guiders themselves, and was proud of their prowess after schooldays, listing in her book 'I was there', the achievements of her 'Old Girls' in Guiding. It was not uncommon for Guide officers to be quite young and famously Loelia Buchan-Hepburn, later Lady Somervell, Headgirl in 1915, became a Commissioner shortly after leaving school. At 19 years old she was Chief Commissioner for Scotland and continued in active Guiding until she went to live in India.

These girls evidently emerged from school well prepared to run a Guide Company and, like Mary Court, able to train others and to receive respect from girls who had been at work for several years, the school leaving age being then fourteen.

The book shows that these girls, working in a glove factory, find Guiding inspiring, bringing colour into their lives. Hetty Thwaite, who is self-centred, vain and bored, for a time is a better person, helping her family and others.

However when her picture appears in a newspaper and she is offered a part in a film, all this is forgotten and she leaves to follow her dream.

Was this typical of the time? Well, Gracie Fields rose from humble beginnings, working in a mill and became a famous actress and well loved person, so no doubt it could and did happen. I do not think even 'Our Gracie' would have risen to such dizzy heights without a good helping of talent and a willingness to learn, none of which Hetty Thwaite apparently has.

The whole experience goes to her head and as the proverb goes 'pride came before a fall!'

A kind doctor helps her, and a nun nurses her to health, finding her a Guide friend in a foreign land. When she travels home she cares for the Italian Guide Leader, who is seasick and returning to London, and is met by Mary Court and her own mother and Guide Patrol. She apologises for the way she has behaved and is forgiven.

The story is somewhat far-fetched to our modern eyes, but I do believe that the way it represents Guiding then is a truthful one and in keeping with the Tenth Guide Law presents the behaviour to which a Guide of the 1920s did aspire.

Chapter 14

Schoolgirl Fiction mentioning Guides

I cannot finish a book with reference to Guide fiction stories without mentioning two of my favourite authors of schoolgirl stories, Elinor Brent-Dyer and Elsie Oxenham. There are a number of book enthusiasts' clubs today, both for these and for other popular authors. I belong to two of these, the 'Friends of the Chalet School' and the 'Elsie Jeanette Oxenham Appreciation Society' both of which issue magazines. These societies, and their enthusiastic administrators and members who contribute to their magazines, have helped keep the work of these authors alive. Also Girls Gone By Publishers have reprinted the books in splendid editions with commentaries and additional information, which has allowed collectors to read the original stories without them having been abridged. Over the years I have enjoyed being a member of both and the friendship and fun this has involved - rather like being a Guide in fact!

The Chalet Girls in Camp - by Elinor Brent-Dyer

Elinor Brent-Dyer has written many books but is mainly remembered for the Chalet School Series, set in a girls boarding school in its different locations, beginning in Austria. She was born as Gladys Eleanor May Dyer in South Shields in 1894 and died in September 1969.

She was brought up by her mother, her father having left them, and was privately educated. She taught for some 36 years from the age of 18, at first as an unqualified teacher. She taught in many different schools throughout the country, state and private, spending periods in further study for a teaching qualification in Leeds and at the Newcastle Conservatoire to further her interest in music.

Later she worked in Hereford as a private governess and, from 1938 to 1948, she had her own school, 'The Margaret Roper School' there.

She moved to Redhill in Surrey in the 1960s and died there in 1969.

Among her interests were folk dancing, Guides and choir and she is probably the most well known writer of girls' school stories.

'The Chalet Girls in Camp' is a story about the Chalet School Guides and was published in 1932 by Chambers. My edition is dated 1955. The Guides' way of camping will be familiar to all those involved in Guiding prior to about 1960, and some of it to those after that date!

The book begins with some of the girls who are living at 'Die Rosen', the home of Madge Russell, founder of the 'Chalet School' in Austria, out blueberry picking. It continues through the brief visit of the King of Belsornia to see his daughter, Princess Elisaveta, prior to her joining in the school's Guide Camp during the school holidays in August. Madge's sister, Joey Bettany (or Jo), is her great friend and the Princess has had some time at the Chalet School.

The excitements of Guide camp, from a prized logbook and an unknown artist

A few days later after a Saturday of thunderstorms, then sunshine, they spend Sunday first going to Mass. In the afternoon they go to visit Gisela Mensch, as Gisela Marani the first head-girl of the Chalet School, and other members of her family, including Joey's great chum, Frieda:

> The next day was Monday, and they spent it in getting ready for their camp. Palliasse covers were brought out and inspected, and pillows were packed into them, as well as changes of clothing, horn tumblers, enamelled plates, knives and forks and spoons, blankets, one or two books in case there should come rainy days, brushes and combs and sponges and soap, and all the hundred and one articles that would be necessary.

On the day of Camp, Joey Bettany, Princess Elisaveta, Grizel Cochrane and Frieda Mensch walk down the mountain to meet some of the other Guides. They are rowed across from the landing stage at Buchau to meet more of the Guides and their Guiders at Briesau, the main village on the lake. The Guiders are Miss Wilson, Miss Nalder and Miss Stewart, all Chalet School Mistresses.

They then go by boat to Scholastika and then by charabancs (coaches) to the Baumersee, a lake on the slopes of the western mountains.

The journey to their campsite goes past farms and through forests until they have to leave the charabancs, as they cannot drive any further. They carry their knapsacks and belongings through the woods and arrive at the Baumersee, a peaceful lake in the mountains, with only a few farms and a small village a short distance away.

There are lots of camp chores to be done, fetching water from a nearby spring, collecting wood for the fire, and unpacking hampers and baskets. Groundsheets are laid to sit on and 'American- cloth' for tablecloths, then they are to eat a meal of sandwiches and fruit brought with them. The girls, bringing wood, return, and it is used straight away, Frieda saying it will be enough for a while:

> "But not nearly enough to last the afternoon." Added Miss Stewart, as she came across to them, carrying a large can of milk. "You will need a great deal more then that, girls."
>
> Simone sighed. "I wish wood did not burn away so quickly. Shall we go and get some more, Madame?"
>
> "No; I think that Frieda is right, and it will do for the present," said Miss Stewart.

Two dixies (cooking pots) are set on the fire, containing milk and water to make coffee, and bread and butter and cake put ready. After a Latin grace is said they sit to have their meal, and Grizel upsets Jo with a remark which gives rise to comment from the adults. Jo is the head-girl, and they feel that Grizel shouldn't have spoken to her as she had in front of the younger girls. Grizel is older and will be on the Staff in the annexe to the school, and they decide to ignore what happened, rather than scold her now.

Bell tents
And one very
Small ridge tent.

Miss Wilson blows her whistle for attention and organises the putting up of the tents:

"Come along, girls," she said, when they were all within earshot. "We've got to get these tents up, and you've had a good rest now. Let me see; there are four tents to hold six each. Two to hold three; two for two; and my own. Then there's the big tent for the commissariat (store-tent), and the spare one for sitting in if it rains. They must all be up tonight as well as all the rest of the camp buildings. Which of you people have learned how to pitch a tent?"

All the elder girls knew, and most of the younger ones had helped during the little weekend camps they had had during the previous term. They divided themselves into parties, and soon were busy at work, digging holes for the centre-poles. The two big tents for the commissariat and recreation tents had ridgepoles, and the Captain judged it best to attend to them herself, with the other two Guiders, Juliet and Grizel, to help.

Jobs are found for the rest, including seeing to the fire, opening out the canvas, setting up the poles, knocking in pegs and fixing the guy-ropes.

An hour and a half later the tents are all up and nearer the lake the two flagpoles, where the flags will be run up at six o'clock the next morning and where Prayers will be taken by the commandant (person in charge of the camp). The campfire site is ready and the incinerator for rubbish sited some distance away.

At some stage too the girls will have had to put their bedding ready, unpacking and finding places for their belongings. Straw will have to be fetched to stuff the palliasses for mattresses.

After more coffee and washing up, the Guides have a rest and, later, will be allowed to bathe in the lake:

"It's half-past four now, so that means we go in at half-past five. Only a short bathe today, as we're so late, so I shall call you out when you have been in a quarter of an hour."

The girls enjoy being in the lake, which, unlike the Tiernsee by their school, is a warm lake, and are promised a longer dip the next day. Back in camp there are more jobs to be done, looking for wood for the fire, fetching water and going to the farm for butter, milk and eggs.

Juliet has forgotten to bring cocoa and they have to drink hot milk instead:

"Then, as we haven't to bother with making cocoa, we'd better go out and see about getting the milk poured out," said Grizel, leaving the tent as she spoke.

Jo followed her, and Juliet was left alone with Miss Stewart. "I'm so sorry, Madame, I can't think how I came to be such an idiot. It's not even as if it were a small tin, that you could overlook - it isn't!

"Never mind," said Miss Stewart. "We can't expect everything to go like clockwork all the time. Come along, Juliet, and don't pull such a long face. The girls must learn to take vicissitudes as well as joys. Come - 'A Guide laughs and sings on all occasions,' you know. And it might have been worse. It might have been something really important - like the hams, for instance, or the jam."

At campfire the Guides are singing and people from the farms creep up to hear them. After Prayers the Guides go to their tents:

Meanwhile, the big storm lanterns had been lighted in the tents and the girls were undressing rapidly.

"I don't believe I'll ever stay on that thing," said Elsie Carr, as she surveyed her somewhat corpulent palliasse with its stuffing of straw.

"I told you you'd put far too much in," said Margia, who was now in her pyjamas and preparing to say her prayers. "You'd better take some of it out."

With a deep sigh Elsie finished her undressing, and then began to do as she was told. She was still at it when 'Lights out' rang out, and the others had to come hastily to the rescue. After something like a scrimmage they got the thing right, and Elsie lay down and began to fold her blankets over her. When Miss Wilson came to the tent it was in darkness, and the girls were all tucked up more or less comfortably. She flashed her electric torch over each one, and made sure that they were comparatively safe from rolling out during the night. Then she wished them 'Good-night!' and withdrew to the next tent. Five minutes later, as the girls were still murmuring to them selves and giggling, 'Taps' sounded, sung by the three Guiders, Juliet, Grizel and the four cadets (older girls training to be Guiders).

We filled palliasses with straw!

162

Joey has brought her dog, Rufus, to camp and there is panic in the night, when he smells a scent from the commissariat- tent (store tent) and goes to investigate. The intruder is a farm dog, which he chases away.

Among other memorable incidents, there is the sensation caused by Cornelia Flower, out gathering wood, who pulls a large piece of green wood through the undergrowth, scratching herself. Green wood, as every good Guide knows, is no use for the fire, as it will smoke and drip sap!

Also Joey, while out wooding, falls down a pit in the ground and is pulled out by Miss Wilson after a noteworthy example of how not to talk to your Guide Captain or a Mistress:

> Miss Wilson went forward to stop, just in time, on the brink of a large hole, surrounded at the edges with piled-up leaves, pine needles, pinecones, and other forest debris. She swirled it about with her axe, in order to discover how much of it had a good foundation, and was rewarded by hearing Jo's voice say, with decided crossness in its tones,
>
> "When you're *quite* done trying to play robin to the babes in the wood, perhaps you'll pull your self together and help me to get out of this!"
>
> "Joey!" cried the Guider, relief in every accent. "Are you quite all right dear? No bones broken or anything?"
>
> Jo declared afterwards that she simply hadn't recognised Miss Wilson's voice, or she never would have replied as she did, "For Heaven's sake stop maundering and use your wits and HELP ME TO GET OUT!"

Miss Wilson takes this in good part and organises Jo's rescue, although, when Jo realises how rude she has been, she makes a heartfelt apology.

One early morning the Guides go fishing and return scared, as they have hooked a body! Local farmers search the lake and find only a model figure, used by an artist and disposed of in the river.

On another occasion Dr Jem Russell, Joey's brother-in-law, and Dr Jack Maynard are on their way to the camp and met by two Guiders. Giving them a lift, they find the camp deserted and can hear 'a humming and a buzzing.' The Guides are hiding in their tents, some of them having disturbed a nest of hornets! The doctors and Guiders manage to escape by car and to find a farmer to kill the hornets.

On one expedition from camp they climb up the Gesslerhorn, going at first up a grass-clad hill and, on the way down, Joey leads the others in sliding down the slope, and Jo and her friends are scolded by Miss Stewart. That night Jo, Marie and Frieda have not yet fallen asleep after the excitements of the day, and hear the rain start to fall. They go out in gumboots, raincoats and sou'-westers to loosen the guy-ropes and go to all the tents as it seems everyone else is fast asleep. Miss Wilson makes them jump, when she calls out to see what is happening. They tell her and she is pleased with their doing just the right thing and brings them all some hot milk, when they are back in their own tent.

On the Sunday the Guides are carrying out various activities and some are given permission to go back and explore the pit Joey fell into. Juliet and Grizel have planted a package for Jo to find, but she also finds a genuine package hidden there.

Three of the Guides, Elisaveta, Paula and Cyrilla, fall into a pond at the farm and return to camp dripping wet and covered with green weed.

The Quartette of friends, becoming a Quintette when Ilonka Barkocz is about and consisting of Elsie Carr, Margia Stevens, Evadne Lannis and Cornelia Flower, who have been left in camp, have been discussing the fact that most of their hankies and some of their clothes are dirty. When they see how wet the others are, Elsie is concerned and as she knows where the keys to the medicine chest are, she fetches the box and mixes up some medicine. She insists they take it to prevent fever, and although it tastes horrible, they manage to swallow it. It is a mixture of liquids and not surprisingly unpleasant.

The Quintette have been left on the site, to look after it, with the aid of Rufus, and to have *Kaffee and Kuchen* ready for the rest when they return from a ramble. Grizel has been left in charge, but was awake in the night with earache and has gone to lie down for a while. The girls are old enough to be trusted, but now attempt to be helpful by washing the clothes of the three who have been in the pond! These girls have now worn all their clean clothes. Ilonka has a brainwave and decides to do oddments for everyone as they have two hours before anyone returns:

> Sending the forlorn trio to wrap them selves in blankets and bring the least soiled of their garments, the Quintette set to work at once. Elsie set the dixies on the fire, while Ilonka filled them with water, and Evadne fed the flames. Cornelia dashed off to the commissariat-tent in search of soap, and returned with two tablets of coal-tar toilet soap - all she could find. Margia found a knife, and began to cut one tablet into tiny pieces, which she put into one of the buckets. On this they poured hot water as soon as the first dixie was ready, and then stirred it with a stick till the soap frothed up. "It's important to have a good lather," said Elsie in professional tones.

When this was ready they dumped into it a miscellaneous assortment of garments, paying no heed to what was coloured and what was white. Guide overalls, handkerchiefs, underclothes - all went in together!

The outcome is disastrous and, when they realise the colours are coming out of garments and spreading into others, they tip the clothes out on the grass and rinse them and wring them out. The overalls are put out on bushes to dry and they try to boil, then starch, the white things!

When the ramblers return, the Quintette's activities are discovered, as, when coffee is made it tastes of soap, the dixies not having been rinsed out.

Washing dixies thoroughly involves much elbow grease!

The three who have fallen in the pond are told that they will have to take some medicine, to take away the effects of their bath and reveal that they have already been given some by Elsie. The washing activities are revealed, including the starching of hankies, camisoles and a pillowcase. As they dry hard, they are like pieces of board!

"I believe," said Miss Nalder in a shaky voice, "that these things would literally stand by themselves."

It was the only comment passed at the moment. Though 'Bill' (Miss Wilson) found plenty to say later on. The washer-women sadly picked up the results of their activities and carried them solemnly to the lake, where the Captain instructed them to soak the maltreated articles till the starch was out of them once more. Later, she called them together, and forbade them to touch the medicine chest; to dose each other; and to wash garments until they had their Laundress badge. "If you had waited," she concluded. "You would have found out that tomorrow we are having a real washing-day. And you would have learned something about it. As it is, you have simply put us all to a great deal of trouble. And you might have poisoned those three!"

The last day of an eventful camp arrives and they have to clear up and return home.

Perhaps the main Guide Laws illustrated by this story are in two of the incidents mentioned. When Juliet has forgotten to bring the cocoa, Miss Stewart reminds her that 'A Guide sings and laughs on all occasions', slightly changing the correct eighth Guide Law, "A Guide smiles and sings under all difficulties.'

The disastrous laundry incident can relate to the all-important first Guide Law, 'A Guide's honour is to be trusted.' The 'Quintette' have been trusted to remain on watch in camp and to prepare refreshments for those returning from a ramble. Instead they meddle with medicines and nearly ruin a lot of clothes.

Nor have they observed the Seventh Law, 'A Guide obeys orders', or none of this would have happened.

The Chalet Guides in camp or at school clearly practise the fourth Guide

Law, 'A Guide is a Friend to all and a Sister to Every Other Guide.', as the Chalet School has girls of all nationalities, who live and work together in a reasonable state of harmony.

Rest Hour after a tiring morning

Fact or Fiction?

Elinor Brent-Dyer had this book published in 1932 and clearly has some personal knowledge of Guiding at that time. She is thought to have been the Captain of 1st Herefordshire Lone Ranger Company, then a fairly recent branch of Guiding, being set up to allow girls to belong to the Guide Movement, without being able to go to meetings, either because they were at a boarding school with no Guide Company or lived in an isolated place or were maybe in hospital. Their Captain would have corresponded with them and sent out copies of badges to do and how they could complete test work. They may even have met together for a special event.

Elinor Brent-Dyer, as a teacher and writer, was ideal for this role.

She may have been involved in ordinary Guide companies at any of the schools where she worked, as school companies were then widespread.

Researching this locally it is evident, from the frequently changing Guiders at companies in boarding schools, that some of these staff were drafted in by the Headmistress, and may never have been warranted Guiders. Maybe Elinor was one of these ladies, who gave up her free time for a school-based activity, over and above her hours as a teacher.

In 'The Chalet Girls in Camp', their camping rings true, right down to the palliasses they slept on and the camp chores they undertook, but also in the campfires and the singing of 'Taps' outdoors, which still brings shivers to your spine in future years. For many girls Guiding and Camp have always gone together.

I have letters from ladies who were Guides in those days and am quoting a few:

Sheila Browne 1997

Your request in the Malvern Girls' College Old Girls' Association Magazine for news about Guides sent me reminiscing on the Guide Camps I went to, which I loved, and were the real reasons for my remaining a Guide!

I was at Malvern Girls' College from 1934-1941 (went down to Somerset and back!) so I suppose I am only remembering the camps of '35-'38. Once to Great Comberton and climbing Bredon, but then to, I think, Eardiston. I have been looking at the map, and I know it was on the River Teme, near Tenbury Wells, and there was a little weir, the sound of which lulled us to sleep. I have had a great attraction to weirs ever since. We filled our palliasses with straw at the local farm. I think it was before the days of sleeping bags so I suppose we just had blankets. We slept in bell tents and practised square lashing to make shoe racks and hangers for clothes on the central pole.

Loos were trenches (dug in advance) with seats, and fill it in yourself with spare earth.

But the thing I remember most vividly was the wire crossing of the river. There were two thick permanent wires, one for sliding your feet across, and one at shoulder height for your hands. I can't think what was on the other side but we just adored going across. I'm sure today there would be safety regulations preventing it! There was a little beach in the centre of the river where we paddled and swam.

Margaret Jarvis 1997

I think we had four Patrols – certainly a Swallow Patrol, of which I became Patrol Leader, and I believe there was a Wren Patrol.

I joined the Guides in my first term in 1938 and remember going to camp that year, but not in 1939 because of the unsettled situation.

We carried on Guiding during our evacuation to Hinton St. George where we had marvellous opportunities for more outside interests such as tracking, map reading and wildlife and I remember taking part in a singsong in the Lodge there.

Phyllis Russell 1997

    I was a Guide at Malvern in 1924 to 1926. I was in 1ˢᵗ company and we met in the gymnasium of Summerfield House.

    I don't remember much about the meetings except we did a lot of signalling and I know my Morse code today so it was well drilled in! I also remember that awful Morse flag we had to make!

    I was never allowed to camp much to my sorrow , as going back to Suffolk after camp was too difficult, also Guiding was frowned upon by my family.

My own mother camped just once in 1927 or 1928, and told me that the palliasses, when packed with straw, were crawling with insects! I think this experience put her off camping, although she took part in all other Guide activities.

I camped in the late 1950s in old white bell-tents, in which we slept a Patrol of six to a tent, with that heavy centre pole. We never actually dug a hole to sink it into, and I am grateful for that, as being a leggy girl of 5ft. 9ins., the only place I could stand up was in the centre.

You could sleep with heads to the pole, radiating out, or heads to the canvas and feet to the pole. As we had 'gadgets', contraptions made from hazel sticks and string,

Four Guides in 1927/1928 in various uniforms in camp. Two in front in camp overalls. My mother, Eva George, in the dark uniform.

169

on which stood kitbags at night and kitbags and bedding rolls in the day, I preferred head to the pole. That way you were less likely to hit your head! However after a night when a tent was let down and the centre pole fell, we decided heads to the canvas was a little safer!

The other parts of the camp routine ring true, meals eaten sitting on groundsheets laid in a horseshoe shape, with food served by the Mess or Cooks' Patrol at the top. The centre part of the grass was the 'Table' where no one walked, unless they wanted a shout of 'Mind the table!' We certainly had no 'American-cloth' or any tablecloth.

a cheerful Wood Patrol

Gwennie, Betty. Doris, & Violet.

Breakfast.

Camp activities: Collecting wood for the fire and enjoying breakfast

We were familiar with the rule of 'no bathing until an hour after food', in case you had cramp in the water, and we too were desperate on the first day of camp to finish our duties and go for a swim, however short. Seaside camps always meant that jobs were carried out quickly with the promise of a swim.

The incident with Elsie struggling with her bedding is familiar too, although our bedding consisted of a sleeping bag and blanket. Often we would still be getting inside them when 'Light's Out' sounded, although our lights were only torches. Also our Guide Captain came round the tents at night to check all was quiet, and she shone a large torch on our tents to catch the unwary! We would keep low and giggle, then scramble into bed I even sat on a needle once!

At Camp-fire we sang 'here comes Captain with her lamp, riding on a donkey.' cribbing from the Guide Song 'Donkey riding.'

Campfires and 'Taps' sung in the open were as memorable for us as for the Chalet Guides, and we would linger as long as we could around the embers.

Hiding on a 'Wide' game - Sketch from a logbook

The Abbey Girls Play Up - by Elsie J. Oxenham

Elsie Jeanette Oxenham was born on 25th November 1880, in Southport, her real name being Elsie Jeanette Dunkerley. She was one of a family of two boys and four girls, their parents being William and Margery Dunkerley.

Her father worked on newspapers, writing articles, then short stories and later novels, adopting as his name for his own writing the name of John Oxenham.

Elsie spent much of the first half of her life living in the Ealing area, doing secretarial work for her father and becoming his companion, until she was established herself as a writer.

The family moved to Worthing and, after the marriages of the two brothers and the death of their parents, the daughters lived together in pairs. Elsie and her sister, Maida, lived in the Chalet Bungalow, used in some of her own writing. She died in 1960.

Among her interests were folk dancing and the Camp Fire Movement, both of which are included in her books. The Camp Fire Movement, which I believe originates in America, involves members wearing Indian robes and earning honours and taking Indian names, along with the magic of a real campfire.

She wrote series of books with numerous characters, who could be brought into more than one series, and is best known for her Abbey Series, set in a ruined Abbey and its associated Hall, the Abbey being based on Cleeve Abbey in Somerset, a lovely place to visit.

Collins printed this book in 1930 and my copy is the 'Seagull' edition dated 1950.

I am only dealing briefly with this book, which is not predominantly a Guiding Story, although Guiding is included. It has two Guide Leaders, Maribel and Rosalind, as the main characters, along with Cecily, a young girl 'adopted' by their Guides after meeting her while camping on the shore of Lake Annecy in France. They have brought her to England and arranged a school for her and somewhere to live with Sarah.

Cecily longs for artistic things, dance and music, after going to folk dance classes run by Mrs Joan Raymond, owner of the Abbey.

She makes a friend of Sandy, Mrs Alexander, who teaches music in the village, and has played for the dancing when the village pianist was ill. Sandy lives alone, after losing her young husband and then her mother, and has had to teach instead of continuing her studies.

Cecily and her Guide 'guardians' become involved with the Abbey crowd through Mrs Raymond and they meet Lady Jen Marchwood and Lady Joy Marchwood. Lady Joy lost her husband, Andrew, less than a year after inheriting his title, which passed to Lady Jen's husband, Ken. They also meet Maidlin, Joyce's ward, and, much later, Rosamund, another friend, who finally traces Cecily's long lost mother.

Lady Joy has withdrawn from many of her activities, concentrating on her twin girls, but, being musical, has set up a small school for girls who need the chance to study and cannot afford it. This is run by a friend, Betty, who runs a Guide Company, but needs help.

Maidlin, another artistic girl, whose musical talent is for singing, feels she should offer help, but is not keen to do this, being rather shy. She responds to a suggestion from Maribel, involved in Campfire, that she becomes a Campfire Leader and this proves to be the right move for her.

Joy is persuaded into Guiding, firstly through Maribel and Rosalind suggesting this to Jen, then by Jen making the suggestion, even if it upsets Joy:

> "Joy, couldn't you help Betty with her Guides? I know it would need a tremendous effort and real courage to take the first step. But you've plenty of courage. You've shown us that. It's only that you aren't using it just now. You're not, you know," as Joy stood and stared at her in horror.
>
> "I? Guides? Jen, are you crazy?"
>
> "Not a scrap! You'd do it well; you'd be a splendid Captain. The girls would love to have you. Think how proud they'll be!"

Jen uses the persuasive argument that Joy's children will ask why their mummy doesn't do things as other people's mothers do:

> Jen pleaded. "Think how proud Margaret would be, when she becomes a Brownie, of a mother who was a Guide Captain!"

Jen also says that by the time the girls are Guides, Joy will probably be District Commissioner. Joy sees that but shrinks from the idea of herself in uniform. She does think it over however.

After a church service when the Guides parade their flags and she sees two rows of Guides, some of whom are old enough to be Rangers, she decides to walk back with Betty:

> "Your girls looked very smart tonight, Bets. There's a nice crowd of them now."
>
> "Too many," said Captain McLean. "I can't take any more, but there are three Brownies almost ready to fly up to us. We can't keep

them back any longer. I must have more help, but I don't know where to turn. The obvious thing is to move out the seniors and form a Ranger Company. Several of them are very keen. But we haven't a captain for them."

Joy stood and looked at her. "Could I do it, Bets?"

Betty is quick to assure her she can and hears what Jen has said to persuade Joy. Joy says how part of her has always envied Betty and the Brownie Leader when she has seen them at church and has thought what a good time they are having:

"I could be as much thrilled as any of the girls if we had a Ranger Company and our own colours."

The story continues with Cecily, and then her friend Sandy, being offered places at Joy's Music School, and with Rosamund appearing from abroad and the unravelling of the mystery about Cecily's background. She is finally restored to her mother.

Fact or Fiction?

In this instance I do feel that much of this story is pure fiction, however much I am a fan of the Abbey series, which takes you into a different world.

This is one of people living in magical places, although many of them do not start out in a position of privilege. The pivotal characters in the earlier books, Joan and Joy Shirley, cousins, later are the owners of the Abbey and Hall respectively, and their friend, Jen, also plays a large part. They do realise however that with privilege comes responsibility, and in many cases open their hearts and homes to others less fortunate.

I have included this brief reference as it does show how Joy becomes a Guider, for her children's sake, and to help others, as she does with her Music School.

Many women have come into Guiding for much the same reason and, in old minute books there are as many married women's names as those of single ladies.

If any of the Guide Laws are illustrated in this book, it must be the second Law, 'A Guide is Loyal' and the fourth ' A Guide is a Friend to All and a Sister to Every Other Guide.'

The Abbey people and their friends are loyal to each other and always ready to make friends and draw them in to their circle.

Concluding Remarks

Many of the books I have used as illustrations are out of print and it will be quite difficult to trace some of them. There are a number of dealers and indeed specialised bookshops, which will stock some of them, and of course there is the Internet.

My own book collection began in the late 1950's and early 1960's, when I was a Guide. I began collecting more seriously in the 1970's, when I became aware that they were seen less in sales and old bookshops, so many were bought for the equivalent of 25p to £1. You will be rarely buy one today for less than £5, and, if it has a good dust wrapper or illustrations, anything from £8 to £12,with the rare books fetching anything over £50.

Although some are very dated, they are a pleasurable read, and, I feel, an accurate reflection of their times and Guiding at the time. Re-reading these I feel much the same pleasure as when I was a Guide myself.

Bibliography of
GIRL GUIDE FICTION STORIES

1911-1978

Reproduced by kind permission of
Mrs Joan Firth of Cleveland

With a few additions.

No.	AUTHOR	TITLE	YEAR	PUBLISHER
1	ABBOTT, K. Nelson	Camp at Seaview Meadow	1929	Blackie
2	ADSHEAD, Gladys Lucy	Brownies hush	1938	O.U.P.
		Brownies, it's Christmas	1955	O.U.P.
3	ALDIS, Janet	The Campers	1921	
		A Girl Guide Captain in India	1924	Girls' Own Paper
4	ANDERSON, Verily	Amanda and the Brownies	1960	U.L.P.
		Brownies and the Christening	1977	Hodder
		Brownies and the ponies	1965	Brockhampton
		Brownies and the wedding day	1974	Brockhampton
		Brownies and their animal friends	1969	Brockhampton
		Brownies day abroad	1964	Brockhampton
		Brownies on wheels	1966	Brockhampton
		Magic for the Golden Bar (a play)	1953	G.G.A.
		Six turns for Brownies		
5	ARMSTRONG, Vera	Biddy the Brownie	1949	Warne
	(pseud. Of Vera Marshall)	Maris of Glenside	1953	Warne
		Rival Camps	1950	Warne
		Tracks to adventure	1947	Brown, Son & F
		Tracks to the Queens Guide Award	1948	G.G.A.
		Trefoil Tales	1956	
		Twenty Tales	1949	G.G.A.
6	BARCLAY, Vera C.	Campfire yarns and stunts	1932	Brown, Son & F.
7	BATTY, Jane Agnes Staunton	The honour of the Company	1922	Wells, Gardner & Co
8	BEACHAM, Barbara	Tracy of the Pixie Six	1975	Brown, Son & F
9	BLATHWAYT, Jean	Brownie discoverers	1977	Hodder & Stoughton
		Lucy's Brownie road	1970	Brockhampton
		Lucy's last Brownie challenge	1972	Brockhampton
		The Mushroom Girl	1977	White Lion
10	BONNER, Julie	Fix it Six	1964	World Dist.
		Pack of trouble		
11	BRADLEY, Anne	Guides in Hanover Lane	1958	Lutterworth
		Problem Patrol	1957	Lutterworth
		Widening path	1952	G.G.A.
12	BRADLEY, A.W.	Won by pluck	1925	Pilgrim Press
13	BRAMBLEBY, Ailsa	Brownie book	1961	G.G.A.
		Commonwealth Pack story book	1965	Brockhampton
		More tales for Brownies	1964	Brown, Son & F
		Ten tales for Brownies	1960	Brown, Son & F
		Three for pack holiday	1964	Brockhampton
		Three for trouble	1963	Brockhampton
14	BRAZIL, Angela	Captain Peggie	1924	Blackie

15	BREARY, Nancy	It was fun in the fourth	1948	Nelson
16	BRUCE, Dorita Fairlie	Captain Anne	1939	O.U.P.
17	BULCRAIG, E.E.	Pixie and other stories	1945	Stockwell
18	BURGESS, E.M.R.	Cherry becomes international	1946	Stockwell
		Hilary follows up	1939	Blackie
		Ready for anything	1948	Stockwell
19	CADBY, Carine	Brownies in Switzerland	1925	Mills & Boon
20	CALLENDER, Reginald	Pamela, Guide and Captain	1931	Black
21	CHANNON, Ethel Mary	Honour of a Guide	1926	Nisbet
22	CHATWYN, Alys	Two Schoolgirl Guides	1924	Epworth
23	CHAUNDLER, Christine	Amateur patrol	1933	Nisbet
		Bunty of the Blackbirds	1925	Nisbet
		Captain Cara	1923	Nisbet
		Jill of the Guides	1932	Nisbet
		Jill the outsider	1924	Cassells
24	"CHRISTIAN, Catherine"	Baker's dozen	1937	Girls Own Paper
		Big test	1947	G.G.A.
		Bringing up Nancy Nasturtium	1938	Girls Own Paper
		Cherries in search of a Captain	1931	Blackie
		Diana takes a chance	1940	Blackie
		Greenie and the pink 'un	1928	R.T.S.
		Harriet takes the field	1942	Pearson
		Harriet: the return of Rip Van Winkle	1941	Pearson
		Kingfishers see it through	1942	Blackie
		Luck of the Scallop Shell	1929	Brown, Son & F.
		Marigolds make good	1937	Blackie
		Pharaoh's secret	1940	R.T.S.
		Phyllida's fortune	1947	Newnes
		Sally joins the patrol	1948	Blackie
		- next book's reprint		
		Seventh Magpie	1946	Blackie
		School at Emery's End	1944	Pearson
		Schoolgirl from Hollywood	1939	Blackie
25	CLARKE, Linda M.	"Guiders' book of potted stories	1932	Brown, Son & F.
		Tales for Brownies	1930	Collins
		(with E. CARRINGTON)		
26	COLLINS, Freda	Barny and the big house pack	1960	U.L.P.
		Beauty quest book for Brownies	1954	U.L.P.
		Brownies and the Fam-Pig	1964	Brockhampton
		Brownies at No. 9	1936	Harrap
		Brownie year	1957	U.L.P.
		Do my best Brownie book	1960	Brockhampton
		Good turn hunters	1963	Brockhampton
		Pack mascot	1966	Brockhampton

	Pack that ran itself	1955	U.L .P.
	Patchwork pack	1968	Brockhampton
	Pow wow stories	1948	Brockhampton
	Pack tales	1962	U.L .P.
	Shrovetide fair	1960	U.L .P.
	Silent three	1961	U.L .P.
	Woodland Pack	1957	U.L .P.
27 COWPER, Edith Elsie"	Camilla's Castle, a story for Rangers	1928	Blackie
	Haunted trail	1926	Blackie
	Wild Rose to the rescue	1921	Sheldon
	Corporal Ida's floating camp	1920	S.P.C.K.
28 DARCH, Winifred	Cecil of the Carnations	1924	O.U.P.
	Cicely Bassett Patrol Leader	1927	O.U.P.
	Gillian of the Guides	1925	O.U.P.
	Poppies and prefects	1923	O.U.P.
	Winifred Darch Omnibus	1936	O.U.P.
29 DAVIDSON, Helen Beatrice	Adventurers in camp	1935	Sheldon
	Ardice for tune	1926	Sheldon
	Belle joins the Brownies	1932	Blackie
	Billy goes to camp	1937	Sheldon
	Brenda in Belgium	1934	Sheldon
	Bridget and the dragon	1927	Nelson
	Brownie Village	1935	R.T.S.
	Bunch a Brownie	1927	Blackie
	Camp across the road	1927	Sheldon
	Castle tea garden	1930	Sheldon
	Geraldine a Ranger	1926	Nelson
	Gipsy Brownie	1933	R.T.S.
	Girl Guide Omnibus	1933	Sheldon
	Guides make good	1925	Sheldon
	How Judy passed her tests	1936	Sheldon
	Jane the determined	1929	Nelson
	Jerry, Joan etc. a Brownie story	1927	Sheldon
	Makeshift patrol	1932	Sheldon
	Meg and the Guides	1928	Sheldon
	Pat of White house	1924	Sheldon
	Peggy Pemberton - Brownie	1923	Sheldon
	Peggy's school pack	1925	Sheldon
	Sea Rangers of Rodney	1933	Sheldon
30 "DYER, Elinor M. Brent"	Carnation of the Upper Fourth	1934	R.T.S.
	Chalet girls in camp	1932	Chambers
	Chalet School and the island	1950	Chambers
	Chalet School and Jo	1931	Chambers
	Judy the Guide	1928	Nelson
	Princess of the Chalet School	1927	Chambers
	Rebel at the Chalet school		

		Rivals of the Chalet School	1929	Chambers
31	EWING, Mrs J.H.	Brownies and other stories	1932	Bell
32	FIELD, Margaret C.	Cecile at St. Clares	1929	Warne
33	FORREST, Carol	Fortune's Coin	1945	Lutterworth
	(pseud of Margaret Tennyson)	Patteran patrol	1944	Pearson
		Quest of the Curlews	1947	Pearson
		Two rebels and a pilgrim	1945	Pearson
34	GAUNT, Penelope	Kitty goes to camp	1932	Sheldon
35	GILLIONS, Ethel	The double fours	1936	R.T.S.
36	GILMOUR, Patience	Cygnets sail out	1943	Lutterworth
		Quest of the wild swans	1941	Lutterworth
		Seven wild swans	1936	R.T.S.
		Three's a company	1935	Girls Own Paper
37	GIRVIN, Brenda	Betty the Girl Guide	1921	Milford
		Girl Scout	1913	Hodder & S.
		June the Girl Guide	1926	Milford
38	GLYN, C.	Unicorn Girl		
39	GREEN, V.M.	Joan to the rescue	1928	Brown, Son & F.
40	GREGORY, Constance	Castlestone House Company	1918	Pearson
41	HANLEY, Phyllis	Bridget of the Guides	1927	Pearson
		Girls grit	1926	Epworth
		Winning her way	1924	Epworth
42	HANN, Mrs. A.C.O.	All about a Brownie	1928	R.T.S.
	(Dorothy)	Brownie from the caravans	1933	R.T.S.
		Brownie Revels (with S.B.Owsley)	1931	Shaw
		Captain	1934	R.T.S.
		Captain Peg	1928	R.T.S.
		David and Jean	1948	Mowbray
		Guides Kitbag (with S.B.Owsley)	1931	Shaw
		It's fun in the Guides	1951	Lutterworth
		June runs the Company	1932	Shaw
		Lieutenant	1935	R.T.S.
		Lifes calling	1936	R.T.S.
		More fun in the country	1947	Lutterworth
		Pam's patrol	1951	Partridge
		Peg and her company	1929	R.T.S.
		Peg junior	1931	R.T.S.
		Peg Lieutenant	1927	R.T.S.
		Peg the Ranger	1924	R.T.S.
		Peg's babies	1931	R.T.S.
		Peg's patrol	1924	R.T.S.
		Pluck of the coward	1926	Black
		Red headed patrol	1936	Girls Own Paper
		Rhoda the rebel	1925	R.T.S.

		Smiler Girl Guide	1925	R.T.S.
		Sunshine Shop	1927	Black
		Ten little Brownie girls	1934	R.T.S.
		Three Guides adventuring (with S.B.Owsley)	1934	Shaw
		The torch bearer	1938	R.T.S.
		What the Brownies did	1930	R.T.S.
		What happened to Peg	1932	R.T.S.
43	HAVERFIELD, Eleanor Louisa	Happy Comrade	1920	Milford
44	HAYES, Nancy M.	Caravan patrol	1926	Cassell
		Guides of Calamity Hill	1925	Cassell
		Meg all alone	1925	Cassell
		Plucky patrol	1924	Cassell
		Tracked on the trail	1925	Sheldon
		Billy, Lone Scout		Nelson
45	HERBERT, Joan (pseud of J.D.Lewis)	First time Jennifer	1959	Lutterworth
		Just an ordinary company	1939	Pearson
		Lorna's first term	1932	Sheldon
		One's a pair	1939	Black
		Penelope the particular	1939	Pearson
		A tenderfoot's A B C	1940	Brown
		Three halves	1936	R.T.S.
		Trail of the Blue Shamrock	1937	R.T.S.
		With best intentions	1935	R.T.S.
		Wrights are left	1938	Black
46	HUDDY, Delia	Blackbirds barn	1965	Constable
47	IRVINE, A.M.	Guides at Cliffe House		
		Naida the tenderfoot	1919	Partridge
		Norah the Girl Guide	1913	Partridge
48	JOHNSON, Cris	Rising of the Larks	1960	Collins
49	JOLLY, Susan	Marigold becomes a Brownie	1957	
50	KEITH, Felicity	Oakhill Guide Company	1933	Blackie
51	KITCHIN, L.Harcourt	Brownie Margaret	1924	Pearson
52	LAKE, Edna	Mystery of Tower House School	1929	Warne
		Peewit patrol	1927	Wells, Gardner Darton
		Serena & the Seventh		
53	LANE, M.S,	Campfire yarns (Editor)	1923	O.U.P.
		Joan of the Brownies	1928	O.U.P.
		Just Peggy	1925	Milford
		Meg of the Brownies	1923	O.U.P.
		More campfire yarns	1925	Milford
		Tales for Brownies (Editor)	1927	O.U.P.

54	LEAN, Mary	Joan of Glen Garland	1934	Girls Own Paper
55	LENNARD, Lady Selina Nellie	Stories on the Girl Guide laws	1932	Scott
56	LLOYD, Joanna	Betty of Turner House	1936	Hutchinson
		Catherine goes to school	1945	Blackie
57	LYNCH, Theo	Adventures of the East Mere Guides	1937	Partridge
58	McGARRY, Kevin	Blue goose East	1965	World Dist.
		Monkey puzzle	1965	World Dist.
59	MANSELL, C.R. (pseud of E.M.Payne)	Curlew camp	1954	Lutterworth
		Littlest Guide	1949	Lutterworth
		Ragtail patrol	1948	Black
		Swallows see it through	1955	Lutterworth
60	MARCHANT, Bessie	Norah to the rescue	1919	Blackie
61	MARSHALL, May	Twenty six guide stories	1935	Sheldon
62	MARSHALL, Vera	Quest of the sleuth patrol	1931	Cassells
63	MAY, Brenda	Lenderhand Brownies	1973	Brown, Son & F.
64	METHLEY, Violet Mary	Bunyip Patrol (Australian)	1926	Pilgrim
		Ensign Lydia Goff	1930	Blackie
		Mystery camp	1956	Blackie
		Windmill Guides	1931	Blackie
65	MIDDLETON, Ivy F.E.	Adventures of the Scarlet Pimpernel Patrol	1937	Sheldon
		Challenge for the Poppies	1965	Victory Press
		Chris Temple patrol leader	1964	Victory Press
		Fourth musketeer	1940	Lutterworth
		Kay of the Pimpernels	1938	Girls Own Paper
		Musketeers and Wendy	1941	Lutterworth
		Poppies and Mandy		
		Red Trefoil	1944	Lutterworth
		Triumphant Pimpernels	1939	Lutterworth
66	MIDDLETON, Margaret	Guide camp at Herons Bay	1927	Blackie
		Guide adventurers	1929	Blackie
		Island camp	1935	Blackie
67	MOORE, Dorothea	Adventurers two	1929	Sheldon
		Brenda of Beech House	1927	Collins
		Greta of the Guides	1922	Partridge
		Guide Gilly adventurer	1922	Nisbet
		Judy lends a hand	1932	Collins
		Judy patrol leader	1930	Collins
		Sara to the rescue	1934	Collins
		Terry the Girl Guide *	1912	Nisbet
		* the first Guide story book ever published		
68	MOSS, Robert Alfred	Challenge book of Brownie stories	1969	Purnell
		Challenge book of Guide stories	1969	Purnell

		Golden bar book of Brownie stories	1961	Brown, Son & F.
		Golden ladder book of Brownie stories		
			1963	Brown, Son & F.
		Venture book of Brownie stories	1969	Purnell
		Wild White pony, a Guide story	1976	Collins
		The Second Challenge book of Brownie stories		
			1981	Starfish Books
69	MOSSOP, Irene	Hilary leads the way	1933	Warne
70	MUMFORD, Elizabeth	Judy joins the Jasmines	1934	C.S.S.M.
71	NASH,	Audrey at school	1925	Sheldon
	Frances Olivia Hartopp	Audrey in camp	1923	Sheldon
		Audrey the Sea Ranger	1931	Sheldon
		Guides of Glen School	1948	Warne
		Hopefuls adrift	1936	Sheldon
		How Audrey became a Guide	1922	Sheldon
		Kattie of the Balkans	1931	Warne
		Lucy of the Sea Rangers	1943	Blackie
		Merrie Brandon	1931	Warne
		Merrily makes things move	1942	O.U.P.
		(with D.Hann)		
		Richenda and the mystery girl	1928	Sheldon
		Richenda in the Alps	1936	Sheldon
		Rosie the pedlar	1925	Sheldon
		Second class Judy	1952	Warne
		Some Brownies and a boggart	1924	Sheldon
72	NORRIS, Phyllis I.	Mystery of the white ties	1937	Sheldon
73	O'FERRELL, Ronald	Brownie fairy book	1921	Sowler
74	OHLSEN, E.E.	Pippa at Brighton	1937	Nelson
		Pippa at home	1940	Nelson
		Pippa in Switzerland	1938	Nelson
75	OWSLEY, Sibyl Bertha	Andy a Pixie	1932	Harrop
		Brownie gold	1939	Lutterworth
		Brownies all	1936	Blackie
		Dulcie captains the school	1928	Sampson Low
		Guides of North Cliff	1925	Blackie
		Madcap Brownie	1929	Blackie
		A make believe Brownie	1929	Nelson
		Nicolette goes Guiding	1939	Blackie
		Round the year Brownie book	1937	Girls Own Paper
		School Knight errant	1934	Shaw
		School that was different	1932	Shaw
76	OXENHAM, Elsie Jeanette	Abbey girls on trial	1931	
		Abbey girls play up	1930	Collins
		Camp mystery	1932	Collins
		Tuck shop girl	1916	

		Freda joins the Guides (short story)	1931	
		Jinties Patrol	1934	Newnes
		Divided Patrol	1992	
77	PARES, Diana	Guides of Fairley	1936	Epworth
		Hawthorn Patrol	1930	Blackie
78	PEPPARD, Tess	The Seven Robins	1930	Sheldon
79	POCOCK, Doris Alice	Kengarth Brownies	1928	Nisbet
80	POLKINGHORNE, R.& M.	Brownies at play	1917	Harrap
		Brownies by the sea	1917	Harrap
81	PROUT, G.	Sea Rangers at Sloo	1949	Blackie
82	PYKE, Lillian M.	Lone Guide of Merfield	1925	Ward Lock
		Phyl of the camp	1918	Ward Lock
83	RHODES, Kathyln	A schoolgirl in Egypt	1937	Harrap
84	RICHARDSON, Dorothy	Wait till I tell you the story of the Irish		
		Brownies	1969	Brown, Son & F.
		The Brownie Adventurers	1983	Knight Books
		The Brownie Explorers	1984	Knight Books
85	ROWE, Mrs. J.G.	Girl Guides of St. Ursula's	1925	Pilgrim Pr.
86	ROWE, Maud	Guides of Pexton School	1927	London Lib.
87	ROYCE, Marjory	Eileen the Lone Guide	1922	Harrop
88	SCOTT, Nancy	Brownie Guides	1978	Ladybird
		Girl Guides	1980	Ladybird
89	SHAW	Guides Kitbag		
90	SMITH, Margaret Scott	Guide Margery	1931	O.U.P.
91	SOWERBY, M.	Guides and Brownies		O.U.P.
92	STITCH, Wilhelmina	Brownies & Guides book of rhymes	1932	Methuen
93	SYKES, Pamela	Air day for the Brownies	1968	Brockhampton
		Brownies and the fire	1970	Brockhampton
		Brownies at the zoo	1969	Brockhampton
		Brownies in hospital	1974	Brockhampton
		Brownies on Television	1972	Brockhampton
		Brownies throw a party	1976	Hodder
		Juliet joins the Guides		
94	TALBOT, Ethel	Betty and the Brownies	1934	Warne
		Betty at St. Benedicks	1924	Nelson
		Brownie Island	1935	Warne
		Brownie Pack and other good turn stories		
			1932	Epworth
		Brownies all	1931	Warne
		Brownies at St. Brides	1928	Warne
		Camp in the wood	1926	Epworth
		Fairy tales for Brownie folk	1933	Epworth

			1938	Pearson
		Guides luck	1938	Pearson
		Island camp	1923	Sheldon
		Jan at Island School, a Sea Guide story		
			1927	Nelson
		Jill, Lone Guide	1927	Pearson
		Neighbours at School	1923	Nelson
		Patricia prefect	1925	Nelson
		Paul and Pam	1933	Warne
		Peggy's last term	1920	Nelson
		Peppercorn patrol	1929	Cassell
		Ranger Jo	1929	Pearson
		Ranger Rose	1928	Pearson
		Rangers and strangers	1938	Nelson
		Sea Rangers All	1935	Warne
		Sea Rangers holiday	1937	Warne
		Skipper and Co.	1929	Warne
95	TAYLOR, Marjory	Priors Island	1939	Blackie
		With the Speedwell Patrol	1938	Blackie
		The Highland School	c1930	Epworth
96.	TEETGEN, A.B.	Open patrols: a story for Catholic Guides		
			1925	Heath Cranton
97	TRAVIS, Falcon	Tawny talent	1966	Brockhampton
		Tawny trail	1967	Brockhampton
98	TYACKE, R.	Round our totem tales for Brownies	1929	N.S.S.U.
99	TYRRELL, Mabel L.	Enchanted camp	1930	Nelson
100	WALMSLEY, Elizabeth	Mary Court's Company	1925	Pilgrim Pr.
		The Wishing Chair		
		Watersmeet		
101	WHITE, Constance M.	Kay of the Kingfishers	1955	Hutchinson
102	WHITE, Heather	Daffodil Row	1937	R.T.S.
		Extravagant year	1929	Brown, Son & F.
		Kerry Blue	1932	Pearson
		Shirley's patrol	1930	Triad
		Sally's silver spoon		
103	WHITE, Madge Torrence	Chum, the new recruit	1928	Warne
		Puck of the Priory Guides	1935	Hutchinson
		The twins of Torborough Camp		
104	WILLIAMS, Ursula M.	For Brownies, stories and games for the Pack		
			1932	Harrap
		More for Brownies	1934	Harrap
105	WILSON, B.M. & Baume, Y.S.	Brownie Secrets	1942	Warne
106	WYLD, D.	Girl of Queen's Mere	1950	Blackie
107	WYNNE, M.	Bobbety the Brownie	1930	Warne

Camping of the Marigolds		Marshall M. & S.
Girls of the Pansy Patrol	1931	Aldine
Guides honour	1929	Warne
Two and a chum	1924	Pearson
Two girls in the Hawks den	1930	Pearson

Additions to above

108	COCHRANE, Carol	Shamrocks for Janith		Epworth
109	FOREST, Antonia	Autumn Term	1948	Faber
110	FRIGOUT, R. de B.	The Smugglers Hole	c1930	Epworth
111	KIPLING, Rudyard	Land & Sea tales for Scouts and Guides		
			1923	Macmillan & Co
112	PAGE	The Three Elizabeths		
113	SHREWSBURY, Mary	All aboard the Bundy		Pilgrim Press
114	SYKES, Pamela	Juliet joins the Guides		

Included but not Guide stories

14	BRAZIL, Angela	Captain Peggie	1924	Blackie
16	BRUCE, Dorita Fairlie	Captain Anne	1939	O.U.P
25	CHRISTIAN, Catherine	Phyllida's fortune	1947	Newnes
44	HAYES, Nancy M.	Tracked on the Trail	1925	Sheldon
52	LAKE, Edna	Peewit patrol (Scout book)	1927	Wells Gardner Darton
60	MARCHANT, Bessie	Norah to the Rescue	1919	Blackie
67	MOORE, Dorothea	Adventurers two	1929	Sheldon
99	TYRRELL, Mabel L.	Enchanted camp	1930	Nelson

BOOKS OF SHORT STORIES FOR BROWNIES BY VARIOUS AUTHORS

Blackie's Omnibus of Brownie Stories	c1950	Blackie&SonLtd
Purnell's Book of Brownie Stories	1982	Purnell
Brownie book	1961	G.G.A
Brownie ring	1951	G.G.A
Brownie revels	1932	Shaw

Great book for Brownies	Editor H.Strang		O.U.P
Little book for Cubs and Brownies			O.U.P
Story of Brownie tales		1923	Bell
Tales for Brownies	Basil Blackwell	1927	G.G.A
The best of Brownie Stories		c1978	Purnell

BOOKS OF SHORT STORIES FOR GUIDES BY VARIOUS AUTHORS

A Book for Girls		c1930	Nelson
Big book for Guides	Editor H.Strang		O.U.P
Blackie's Girl Guide Story Omnibus		c1960	Blackie&SonLtd
Book for Guide adventurers		1929	Highway
Bumper Book for Guides		c1928	Collins
Girl Guide book - 3 volumes	Editor M.C.Carey	1925	Pearson
Girl Guide omnibus		1932	Nisbet
Girl Guide stories		1929	Blackie
Girls school bus		1934	Sheldon
Guiding book	Editor A.Kindersley	1923	Hodder & S.
Golden library for Guides and Brownies			Blackie
Stories to tell Scouts and Guides	Editor E.E.Reynolds	1933	Harrop
The Girls' All-Round Book	Editor Mrs Walter Wood	c1930	Nelson
The Guides Kitbag	By E.A.Shearlock		
Kitbag Book			Shaw
Thrilling stories of Girl Guides		1931	Nelson
1st Haversack book	Editor G.M.Place	1956	Blandford
2nd Haversack book			Blandford
1st Rucksack book	Editor T.W.Myers	1953	Blandford
2nd Rucksack book	Editor M.Playle	1955	Blandford
3rd Rucksack book	Editor G.M.Place	1957	Blandford
The First Trail of the Girl Guides		1927	Blackwell
The Second Trail of the Girl Guides		1928	Blackwell
The Guiders' book of potted stories	Editor Linda M. Clarke	1928	Brown, Ferguson Ltd

ANNUALS INCLUDING GUIDING STORIES

Big book for Girls	*Editor Strang*		O.U.P
Collins Girl Guide Annual		c1930	Collins
Empire Youth Annual		1947	
Hutchinsons Girls Annual			
Mrs Strang's Annual for Girls			
Nelsons budget for Girls		1934	
Schoolgirls own annual		1926	
Schoolgirls own annual		1928	
Schoolgirls own annual		1930	
The Girls All Round Book	*Edited W.Wood*		Nelson
The Modern Gift Book for Children	*Edited M. England*	C1950	Odhams Press
The Peal Book of Girl Guide Stories		C1930	Peal Preaa
Worth the effort			
Warne's Top-All Book for Girls	*Editor M.England*	c1930	Warne

Not included - Brownie and Guide Annuals and many non-fiction books